Education for Justice

# Education for Justice

BRIAN A. WREN

ORBIS BOOKS, MARYKNOLL NY 10545

1977

Library of Congress Cataloging in Publication Data

Wren, Brian A        1936-
    Education for justice.

    Bibliography: p.
    Includes indexes.
    1.    Justice—Study and teaching.    2.    Social
justice—Study and teaching.    I.    Title.
JC578.W7        301.24'2'07        77-8698
ISBN 0-88344-110-1

*For Brenda, Hilary and Nicholas*
*who have taught me much about justice*
*and most about love*

# Contents

# *Preface*

Many people have helped me to write this book. The Churches' Committee on World Development (1969–1975) gave me the opportunity to work and think on the issues and time to put thought into writing. Colleagues in Christian Aid, the Justice and Peace Commission, the World Council of Churches and elsewhere gave friendship, support and encouragement, in particular Eric Jay, Erik Pearse, David Millwood, Philip Lee-Woolf and Jackie Lyus, who also typed the final manuscript. Beyers and Ilse Naudé, Peter Randall, Theo Kotze and other South African friends immeasurably enlarged my experience and understanding, including some who might suffer if I named them. Pat Sills pointed me towards some important writings on community development. Rosalind Dean helped me to try and write for the rationalist as well as the Christian. The Trickett, Bunker and Beck families made valuable comments on the first draft, which John Bowden's perceptive eye helped me to condense and sharpen. Though the final result is my own, I owe a critically conscious debt to Paulo Freire for his many insights on knowing, education and conscientization, and to the other writers and sources mentioned below, together with many whose names do not appear. My wife Brenda has been an indispensable partner in working out the meaning of love and justice and helping me to shape it into words, while our two children have helped me to learn the everyday implications of 'justice as fairness' (see chapter 3) and to remember that unlike charity, justice begins at home.

# *Introductory Note*

At every level, from local 'redevelopment' and women's rights to the wealth gulf between nations, justice is now a key issue.

To deepen the awareness of injustice, and awaken ourselves-with-others to action, is an educational task. Anyone who tries to share their concern about such issues with others is engaged in 'education for justice'.

The following pages explore the meaning of social justice and the principles of this type of education. Though written from a Christian standpoint they do not presuppose Christian faith. I hope that they will also be useful to readers whose concern about justice springs from a non-Christian or non-religious conviction.

If what I have written is clear, it may not be entirely comfortable. If the line of argument is sound its political implications are radical. I can only ask the reader to weigh the argument on its merits, test it at every point and, as the book itself suggests, enter into a dialogue.

Because it seemed important to take one theme and pursue it as thoroughly and sharply as possible, I have not attempted to say everything that needs to be said about justice, education or Christian faith. Many of the gaps can be filled by others. Christian readers could usefully set what follows alongside John V. Taylor's, *The Go-Between God* (SCM Press 1972) to place it within a wider vision.

Finally, as a small step towards justice in our language, feminine pronouns include the masculine sense, and vice-versa, except when a particular gender is specified.

# I

# The Act of Knowing

The fundamental question about education is, what is *to know?*
Paulo Freire

What sort of person are you? If you were asked, and guaranteed anonymity, you could probably describe yourself as clearly and sensitively as the people below. The first two are a man and woman in their late thirties:

> I think the starting point of my way of life is to love. But of course it doesn't always work out like that. I try to be fair and kind, though often I'm quite unsuccessful in judging the needs of others. I have a considerable streak of vanity, which can lead to selfishness and therefore provides a conflict with the basic aim. I am a fairly happy person, certainly outwardly, and tend to 'look on the bright side'...

> I am a peacemaker, and a fighter. I like honest relationships. I like people – I like them best if they are real, but I try to accept them as they are. I am perhaps too independent. I like coping with life on my own. But I have a sense of inferiority in most things. I am not good at anything. I should love to be good at something...

The third speaker is a man in his mid-forties:

> I wish I could say I was open, uninhibited and direct. It would be nice to think I was the open book people seem to think I am. But I am an introvert – all too conscious of the pages that lie hidden behind the ones on public view, and of the inconsistencies they contain. I enjoy getting to know other people and exploring relationships, yet frequently feel self-conscious, shy and clumsy. I waver between taking everything as it comes, and becoming panicky and stubborn over the trivial and the unavoidable. I look eagerly to the future, yet have a

niggling fear of life slipping by without my doing anything really
significant. I am patient with people, except on the roads. I am a
committed, convinced Christian with a strong pagan streak. I value
the fruits of technology, yet long for the simple life, the bare neces-
sities. When I draw a picture, I do not pencil clear, bold, simple
lines. I draw confused masses of lines, out of which I then try to make
sense. That is how I feel about this sketch. It is what I see when
I look into myself.

Our three speakers vary considerably in temperament. One
seems happy and outgoing. Another is independent but has a sense
of inferiority. The third is deeply introspective beneath the appearance of *bonhomie*. But the most remarkable thing about them is
so universal that we take it for granted. In common with every other
member of the human race, they can all, as it were, step back
mentally, not only from the outside world, but from their own
personality. They not only *feel* happy, inferior, independent,
clumsy or shy, but can examine and describe such feelings – and
so to some extent stand apart from them. They not only experience inner conflicts, but can name and analyse them – and so
perhaps begin to resolve them. As human beings we can all, like
them, describe 'what I see *when I look into myself*'. We not only
know, but know ourselves, and know that we know.

This capacity for self-consciousness[1] is a distinctive feature of
human life, and transforms the nature of human knowledge. Its
appearance was a decisive step forward in evolution, setting us
apart from the rest of the animal kingdom and making possible
our highest achievements.[2] The three-year-old girl who emerges
from playgroup with a worried-yet-quizzical look saying, 'I've got
problems with myself', has already crossed the great divide. In
philosophical terms, she is, and can increasingly become, a
knowing, self-conscious subject. Her world – of home, parents,
friends, school, streets, and even her own conscious self – becomes
the object of her knowledge.

### *The knower and the known*

Before exploring this further, we must look briefly at the relationship between subject and object, between the 'I' that knows and

the world that is known. At the risk of gross oversimplification, there are four possible ways of seeing this relationship, and it is important to choose between them.

The first two obliterate the distinction, saying either that the world I see is entirely in my own mind (solipsism) or that my consciousness is a mere reflection of reality and has no independent awareness or life of its own (mechanical objectivism). I shall assume that these are alike unconvincing and leave them aside without further discussion. The third possibility is that subject and object, the self and the world it knows, are so separate and distinct that they have no effect on each other. At first sight, this seems quite plausible. Our very language suggests that in the phrase, 'I see you', what I am doing is quite independent of you, and that when I see a spider's web, neither I nor the spider's web is altered by the experience.

Yet on further thought, this interpretation is inadequate. If I come to know the world around me more clearly, I am in some way changed by the knowledge. And the meaning of what I see and know comes from within myself, *from the way that humans see*, not merely from the thing seen. To call a sticky pattern of extruded filaments a spider's web is to name it, classify it, connect it with other sticky patterns, even with other types of spider, and give it its place in a whole world of meanings *created by man*. 'We are *not* saying that there isn't anything out there. We *are* saying that the meaning of what is out there is ascribed to it by a perceiver.'[3] Studies in perception have probed sufficiently far into the mysterious relation between the knower and the known to show that it is a continuous and complex 'bargaining process' between what is inside our skins and what is outside.[4]

The relation between subject and object should therefore be seen as a dialectical relationship[5] between things separate yet bound together, where each changes and affects the other while remaining distinctively itself. To know something is to step back from it, yet also to grasp it, to separate yourself from it in the act of connecting with it, to see it as it really is yet give it a name and meaning that come from within yourself. On the one hand, to quote a Chilean peasant, 'there is no world without men'. For if the human race died out, and the animals, birds, rivers and stars remained, 'there would be no-one to say, this is the world'.[6] On

the other hand, the universe exists in its own right and has structures and patterns of its own. If you go out into the open country
and look around, your horizon is determined by the place on which
you have chosen to stand. You cannot help being the centre of
what you survey. Your vision radiates outwards, and your mind
names and interprets the scenery, giving it meaning and pattern.
The landscape is really there, but the horizon and the pattern are
determined by you, the human subject. Yet sometimes you can
come, say, to a crossroads, or to a watershed between two rivers.
The pattern you make – by looking and naming – fuses with a
pattern that is inherently there. Your eyes are opened, and you *see*.[7]

## Nature and culture[8]

The dialectical relation between the knower and the known gives
human life its distinctive character. Because we can stand back
from the world around us, and consciously reflect upon it, we
can see things as they are, yet also imagine what they could be.
We can plan how to change what we see, and put our plans into
effect. If our child's guinea pig needs to roam around the garden,
we can weigh the alternatives in our mind, and decide whether
to seal the fences or make a portable 'run'. If sealing the fences
would not keep out the neighbour's cat, we can form a rough
mental picture of a strong, covered, manoeuvrable frame, go in
search of wood, netting, tacks and screws, spend a few hours
putting it together, and then put the guinea pig safely out to grass.
The resulting construction may not be a work of art, but neither
is it a work of nature. It is, in anthropological terms, a work of
culture – meaning not the refined wisdom of a 'cultured' minority
but the universal human ability to add something new and original
to the natural world.

Animals, too, produce and make complex and beautiful things.
The bee builds its cells, the spider its web and the bird its nest.
In doing so, however, they follow the pattern of their particular
species, and cannot step outside it. Any change in their inherited
pattern is the slow result of mutation and natural selection, not
of conscious planning. Human beings, however, have almost
limitless possibilities of creation. Spiders can't make honey – but
men and women can and do spin, weave, make ploughs to till

the soil, refine cane into sugar, develop new strains of rice and wheat, send probes to Mars and Venus, and a million other things besides. Animal consciousness is *submerged* in nature – human consciousness *emerges* from nature in order to know it and change it. Animal species adapt to their environment in order to survive. The human species modifies its environment in order to find fulfilment.

### The achievement of critical consciousness

The relation between human beings and their culture is not static or one-way. It is an alternating current in which people shape culture and culture shapes people. When our earliest ancestors made flints, developed language, tamed fire and tanned skins, they created a world of culture. Later generations were born into that world and conditioned by it, yet were able, in varying degrees, to change and develop it in turn – and so on, throughout history.

Each generation, each person, has to emerge again into consciousness of the world in order to become fully human. The world of culture into which we are born is like the atmosphere – complex and all-pervading. It includes our language, social customs, and political and economic structures. It has an invisible network of built-in attitudes: to the family, to work, property and possessions, to authority, to other classes and races and to the nation state. It is a universe of meanings that we absorb, accept, or are taught, from birth and throughout childhood. To become fully conscious of this world we have to emerge from it and inspect what we have absorbed, question what we have accepted, and scrutinize what we have been taught. We have to focus our self-consciousness so that it becomes a *critical consciousness*, continually questioning itself and remaking its interpretation of the world.

The development of critical consciousness is neither automatic nor inevitable. A peasant in Allende's Chile was once asked why he hadn't learned to read or write before the government's land reform. 'Before the agrarian reform, my friend,' he replied, 'I didn't even think. Neither did my friends.' 'Why?' he was asked. 'Because it wasn't possible. We lived under orders. We only had to carry out orders. We had nothing to say.'[9] This peasant had lived under an authority so oppressive that his capacity for critical consciousness had been silenced. He had literally been forbidden to think for himself. Other people, his landowner in particular, would do his thinking for him. In the closed world of the feudal land-holding (*latifundium*) he had grown up utterly dependent on his master, and had absorbed the attitudes of submission, passivity and self-depreciation imposed by that culture – a culture dating back hundreds of years to Spanish colonial times. To emerge from this state of mental slavery was like a rebirth. His emergence was made possible by a combination of political change (land reform) and an educational programme aimed at developing not only literacy but critical consciousness and self-respect.[10]

There are many ways of describing our capacity to hurt and oppress each other. In the terms being used here, we can say that self-consciousness necessarily makes both people and things the objects of our knowledge. It therefore carries with it the possibility of treating both alike, of failing or refusing to recognize other people as self-conscious subjects like ourselves. We can treat them not only as objects of knowledge but as the object of our decisions. On every page of history, and in the most free society, we find attempts to silence people's capacity for critical thought or (more commonly) to allow them to ask only certain kinds of question or think for themselves only within narrow limits. If critical consciousness is a distinctive achievement of human life, we can say that to deny or restrict it in other people is to *dehumanize* them.[11] Conversely, when the Chilean peasant emerged from his enforced silence we could say that he became more of a man, more fully human than he was before. From being the object of his master's decisions, he became a subject. He found his voice, and discovered that he had something to say.

*Cultural oppression and education for justice*

The cultural oppression that stunts people's self-consciousness is not confined to extreme situations like the near-serfdom of a Latin American peasant. It is found whenever people's capacity to think for themselves is restricted, and wherever they are reduced to sub-missiveness, passivity and near-silence by their social environment. A characteristic of our own urban life is a sense of powerless-ness. It is most acutely felt in the poorest areas of the city, whose people cannot reach the subtle levers of power that middle-class citizens take for granted – money, a good address, influence, status, access to lawyers and accountants, ability to write 'official' letters and use the telephone. In such a situation, you have a vote but have probably long since despaired of politics. You probably subsist on a low income or are dependent on Social Security payments. You live in below-standard rented property, and send your children to overcrowded nineteenth-century schools. Little by little, you retreat into silence and depression, the 'apathy' of the urban poor:

> It is common to hear professionals – teachers, planners, clergy, social workers – bemoan the apathy of people. 'They are not interested'; 'They will not help themselves'; 'No one is bothered' – are common comments. . . . *Beneath this apparent cloak of indifference, beneath the protective shell of apathy, there is a deep feeling of futility, of an inability to change anything.*[12]

In other words, people in our deprived areas feel powerless because they see themselves as the object of other people's decisions, as pawns moved helplessly across the urban chessboard in the baffling game of 'redevelopment'. If this is true, one of the key aims of education for justice must be to encourage the development of critical consciousness, so that people emerge from their silence, find their voice, and become fully-conscious subjects, capable of trying to change the conditions in which they live.

## Inside the act of knowing

Self-consciousness gives human life its distinctive character and some of its distinctive problems. It also transforms the nature of human knowledge. The distinctive feature of our learning is not conditioning, skill training or memorization, but *changes in consciousness*. Scientific study of how such processes work is in its infancy. What follows is therefore a brief attempt to understand them from within.

The change of consciousness when we learn something new is unlikely to be purely intellectual. If the new learning directly affects our self-image, our outlook on life, or our deep-seated attitudes and beliefs, it is an emotional experience as well. The emotion can be intensely pleasurable. 'Yesterday I could not sleep', says a Chilean peasant, 'because yesterday I wrote my name.' 'I was happy,' says another, 'because I discovered that I could make words speak.'[13] On the other hand, if the learning experience convinces us (for example) that we have been cheated and fooled, or that we have achieved our comforts at the cost of other people's misery, the discovery is likely to be painful. 'It is always difficult to recognise what has been done to you, when the recognition is itself degrading.'[14] If accepted and followed through such changes will affect our attitudes, our religious and political convictions, and our daily behaviour.

The change of consciousness in the act of knowing seems to be experienced as *something that comes unbidden*, yet also as *something we actively do*. This applies to many different types of learning.

Creative discovery occurs, for example, when two quite separate patterns of meaning or experience suddenly interconnect to form a new pattern. A celebrated instance is Gutenberg's invention of moveable-type printing. Gutenberg started with the then current technique of making playing cards. This involved taking a wooden block, engraving it in relief, inking the block, placing paper on it and rubbing the back of the paper. Since Gutenberg wanted to print whole books, in particular the Bible, his first problem was to find a way of reproducing individual letters, since entire pages of print could not be hand-carved in relief. He got the idea of casting individual letters by analogy with the dies used in making coins, but could get no further. The method of hand-rubbing could not produce a clear or deep enough impression. Having tried various ideas and got nowhere, Gutenberg put the whole problem out of his mind and went on holiday. As he helped to gather in the grape harvest he noticed the strong but steady pressure exerted by the wine press as it was screwed down on top of the grapes. The two previously unconnected ideas came together in a moment of insight, he grasped the idea of a printing *press*, and the discovery was made.[15] The new knowledge came unbidden, and the crucial insight was reached by unconscious processes, not logical inference. Yet the creative connection was made in Gutenberg's own mind, not implanted in him by someone else. It is therefore correct to say that Gutenberg *discovered* this knowledge, not that he was taught or shown.

The American teacher, John Holt, records a similar experience. One bright summer day some friends took him to a school of art and crafts. There, for the first time, he saw a hand loom. All the parts were clearly visible, and as his friends talked knowledgeably about weaving he puzzled over it and tried to reason how it worked. All his attempts at understanding proved fruitless. The repeated explanations of his friends were unhelpful, as was the niggling feeling that a moderately intelligent person *ought* to be able to work it out for himself. In the end he shut out the explanations, silenced the voice within him that kept trying to make deductions and ask questions, and contented himself with simply looking at the machine. After a while the party moved on, and the remainder of a full day's visit included demonstrations of pottery, print-making and glass-blowing. Some hours later they started the long drive home. The conversation was about pottery, and Holt was not consciously thinking about the loom. But something extra-ordinary happened. 'As we talked, a loom began to put itself together in my mind. There is no other way to describe it. Suddenly, for no reason, the image of a particular part would appear in my consciousness, but in such a way that I understood what that part was for.' The understanding was visual rather than verbal: he could not *say* what the part did but could see it doing its work. 'By the end of the day,' he continues, 'a loom had made itself in my mind.' There was much about looms that he didn't yet understand, but he knew where knowledge left off and ignor-ance began, what sort of questions to ask and how to make sense of the answers.[16]

Again, the learning process was largely unconscious. Holt felt that it would have been impeded by conscious reasoning, or even close attention. Although he experienced it as something that happened to his conscious self (the loom 'made itself in my mind') it was nonetheless his own mind that was doing the work. Attempts by well-meaning friends to 'plant' their understanding and explanations had little obvious effect. Instead, they aroused feelings of irritation and anxiety, not usually aids to learning. If we broaden the conception of the knowing subject to mean a person's total mental activity – including unconscious and non-rational thought – it is more accurate to say that John Holt was a subject performing an act of knowing rather than the object of someone else's teaching.

Similar considerations apply to rational thought. If I accept the twin premises that 'all grass is green' and 'this substance is grass' it is in my own mind which draws the conclusion, 'therefore this substance is green'. Any attempt to teach me this type of reasoning will fail if I am not yet ready to grasp it. However many times I am told that this is so there has to be – somehow, one day – an act of knowing within me by which I *see* that it is so. A teacher's skill consists, not in performing this act of knowing for me, but in juggling with different patterns of language, giving concrete examples, and trying different explanations, until one of them makes sense.

Thus, as most teachers would probably now agree, the fact that a child has heard, repeated and memorized the phrase, '$4 \times 4 = 16$', does not necessarily mean that he or she *knows* this in the sense of perceiving the number relationships involved. To understand that '$4 \times 4 = 16$' involves an act of knowing by the child. Here again, the skill of teaching is not to implant this knowledge but rather to try and create the classroom conditions (with coloured rods, building bricks, etc.) in which such acts of knowing can occur.

In both its conscious and unconscious modes then, *knowing is an act performed by a human subject. It is something I do, not something that can ever be done to me or for me by someone else.*

### Knowing and doing

A final point is that learning activity concerned with justice, injustice and the development of a critical consciousness gains its new knowledge as much by action as by reflection. Critical consciousness can only develop if it tacks constantly between practice and theory, like a yacht moving upstream against the breeze. There was once a poverty-stricken woman who had to cope with a mentally-ill husband and a large family. She lived in slum council property, and had no prospect of rehousing in better accommodation because her standard of housekeeping was thought to be too low. The dwelling's outdoor toilet was unusable in wet weather due to holes in the roof. The council made no attempt to repair them, despite the woman's frequent requests. Resigned and passive, she felt that there was nothing she could do but accept the council's decision.

Then she joined the committee of a local neighbourhood association, and started running one of its playgroups. She saw how the committee handled its relations with the council and realized that she herself did not have to be so meek in her dealings with officials in the Housing Department. She adopted a more aggressive pose, asked to see the housing manager, refused to leave the building until her request was granted, and then threatened to go to the press unless the repairs were made. The toilet was quickly repaired.[17]

This woman went through a learning process that alternated constantly between action and thought. First, she acted, by joining the committee of the neighbourhood association. There she learned, by observation, that the committee dealt more confidently with council officials. Her realization that she could be more active in pressing her claim was a further act of knowing. But such 'knowledge' could only be completed and confirmed – *could only be fully known* – by the further action of making a fuss in order to be heard.

In education for justice, then, the old saying – 'I hear and I forget, I see and I remember, I do and I understand' – takes on a new lease of life. It suggests that we can only know justice by doing it, in a unity of action and reflection.

# 2

# Education as Dialogue

Knowledge is produced in response to questions. And new knowledge
results from the asking of new questions ... once you have learned
how to ask questions – relevant and appropriate and substantial
questions – you have learned how to learn and no one can keep you
from learning whatever you want or need to know.[1]

Education is to theories of knowledge as an orchestra to its score.
Performance and interpretation vary widely, but different musical
concepts give quite different patterns of sound. If knowledge is
seen as something fixed – as measurable chunks of 'subject-matter'
or clearly defined habits of thought – then the learner's task is to
absorb it. Its size, shape and content are already decided, and the
problem is how to remember the subject matter or copy the habits
of thought. The educator's task is to pass on the knowledge as
effectively as possible. Though education can include new discovery, its main concern is 'the *preservation* of essential knowledge
... and ... its *transmission* from each generation to the next.'[2]
Education is a ceremony of initiation where a person already
initiated (the teacher) introduces uninitiated people (the pupils)
to the knowledge that society wants them to 'master, know,
*remember*'.[3] It is a one-way relationship, where A (who knows)
tells or shows something to B (who does not know) and where
A is placed over B rather than beside him.

On the other hand, if knowledge is an act of discovery performed by a subject who steps back mentally from her world, if
the distinctive feature of human knowing is the development of
a critical consciousness which questions its culture and itself, and
if everyone has this capacity to know, then education cannot be

regarded as a simple transfer from one person to another. It becomes a joint effort, where A and B together question and investigate the object of knowledge. It becomes a dialogue 'in which everyone knows something but is ignorant of something else, and all strive together to understand more'.[4]

### Problem-posing education: some examples

To see education as a dialogue changes both the methods used and the relation between 'teacher' and 'learner'. If to learn means trying to stand back from the world in order to understand it, then teaching means helping people to gain mental distance from what they have previously taken for granted. If knowing means discovering, questioning and investigating, then teaching means presenting the most apparently obvious of 'facts' as a problem for exploration. The following discussion was tape-recorded in a working-class area of Liverpool during a course on marriage, the family and courtship. The two girl speakers lived in an Educational Priority Area and would be generally regarded as 'below average' or 'educationally deprived'. They were fourteen-year-olds at the local comprehensive school who had no plans beyond leaving at the earliest possible age. The tutor belonged to the Workers Educational Association.

| | |
|---|---|
| TUTOR: | Do you think children should be allowed to do what they want in the home today? |
| 1ST GIRL: | Yes. |
| 2ND GIRL: | Yes. |
| TUTOR: | You do? |
| GIRLS: | Yes. |
| TUTOR: | And what does 'doing what you want' mean for you? |
| 1ST GIRL: | Living your own life. |
| TUTOR: | Living your own life. Now what exactly does 'living your own life' mean? |
| 1ST GIRL: | Well, doing things what you want to do yourself and not what your mum and dad want you to do. |
| TUTOR: | And what sort of things would they be now? |
| 2ND GIRL: | Like staying at home and cleaning up and all that, when you could be out enjoying yourself. |

TUTOR:          You don't think you have any responsibilities
                towards the home and towards your parents?
1ST GIRL:       A fair amount.
TUTOR:          A fair amount. You do think you have certain
                responsibilities?
1ST GIRL:       Yes.
TUTOR:          What shape would these responsibilities take? What
                would this responsibility mean?
1ST GIRL:       Helping out when you can.
TUTOR:          Helping out when you can, if you want to help out.
                You say you have got this responsibility to help out
                when you can yet at the same time you want to do
                what *you* want. How do you resolve that?
2ND GIRL:       Do what you want and help out where you can help
                out when you want to.
TUTOR:          Oh yes I see. You mean that you don't want to be
                told that you should do it?
2ND GIRL:       Yes. Do it of your own free will.
TUTOR:          Do it of your own free will. Well do you think that
                if it is left to the free will of young people that they
                will, in fact, help out?
2ND GIRL:       Yes. [5]

A number of points stand out in this conversation. Firstly, the
Tutor tries to show empathy – he often reflects back what has
been said to him, either verbatim or in slightly different words,
as if to make sure that he has understood, and that the girls know
this. Secondly, his leadership consists almost entirely of questions.
Some of the questions ask for an opinion ('Do you think children
should be allowed to do what they want in the home today?').
Others try to clarify the meaning of the opinion expressed ('What
does "doing what you want" mean for you?'). The questions are
not *test* questions – that is, they do not have a right or wrong
answer, like 'what is the capital of Belgium?' They are *enabling*
questions which the girls can answer out of their own thought
and experience. The continued probing into the meaning of what
has been said gradually clarifies the relationship of freewill and
responsibility in a family setting.

The key question occurs in the middle of the conversation, when the tutor takes two apparently contradictory things that the girls have said and presents them in the form of a question – 'You say you have got this responsibility to help out when you can, yet at the same time you want to do what you want. *How do you resolve that?*' Once again, this is not a test question about 'facts' which the girls may or may not know. It presents part of their own thinking as a problem for investigation. The problem is presented in an open way, and is a serious enquiry, not a gimmick to capture their interest. The question encourages the girls to step back from what they themselves have said, and to reflect on it. It calls for thought rather than the recovery of things remembered.

The tutor is clearly leading the discussion. The method used implies that he is genuinely interested in what the girls have to say, that he takes them seriously as people and regards their thinking and experience as valid and important, that he sees himself as having a basic equality with them in the exploration, and that he himself expects to gain something from it. Though it might be possible to put on such attitudes as a teaching device, it would be impossible to keep up the pretence for long. One may therefore assume that attitudes of respect for people, interest in their thoughts and experience, equality, and a willingness to learn from others are basic to this method of education.

In another example, a class of fifteen-year-old boys is learning about the enclosure movement in England during the late eighteenth and early nineteenth centuries, using a specially designed history game.[6] The game takes several periods of class time. Each person has a workbook which presents the situation of a typical village before, during, and after enclosure. Before enclosure the land is divided into numerous equal-sized strips on the medieval pattern. The first problem is to decide where to site the village, assuming that a wealthy landowner wishes to move it in order to landscape his property. Each player looks at three alternative sites, weighs up the pros and cons of each, then compares his score with the rest of the class in order to arrive at a class decision. Factors to be taken into account in choosing a site include its relative nearness to the common (grazing land for the owners of cattle and sheep), the wood (source of timber, grazing for pigs), the field strips, the stream (water for washing, drinking, cooking and animals), and the road.

Having sited the village, the class members take the roles of different villagers – the squire, rector, yeomen, freeholders and small freeholders. The number of strips each person owns varies according to wealth and social position: the squire has twenty-four, the rector and yeomen have eight each, while the ten freeholders have either four or two. Each person reads the brief description of his role and decides whether he is for or against enclosing the land to form single plots. The roles vary enough to allow different decisions within the same social structure. Thus, the two yeomen have different attitudes to enclosure despite the economic advantages they would both stand to gain. Factors to be taken into account include the benefits of new farming methods (for those who can afford them), the possibility of cultivating more land, the cost of enclosure (prohibitive to the smallest freeholders) and the probable bias of the Enclosure Commissioners in favour of the squire, rector and yeomen. The class members take part in a 'parish meeting' to argue their case and announce their decisions. The votes are counted, and the village decision assessed in accordance with the Enclosure Act of 1801.

The game then moves on a number of years, and assumes that the village has now decided in favour of enclosure. The players take on the role of Enclosure Commissioners deciding how to divide up the land, then tackle the problem of the freeholders deciding where to site their houses on the new plots. The resulting map of the village is then compared with the map before enclosure.

The enclosure game is designed, not to present information but to help people organize concepts. It does not tell the detailed story of enclosure, nor even of an actual village. Instead, it helps the players to enter into the typical problems which thousands of villagers had to face, and the range of alternative choices open to them. The game assumes that the experience people gain by playing it is relevant for education. It tries to present history, not externally, as a set of frozen facts, but from the inside, as a process growing from the interplay of economic change with human decisions. The concepts and experience gained are intended to help the players make more sense of historical information about enclosure – to make history textbooks come alive. Having taken part in this particular game I can testify to its effectiveness: I learned more about the English agricultural revolution from ten minutes' playing time than from the reading of several books.

Such games provide many opportunities for a problem-posing method. Whether the opportunities are taken or not depends on the teacher's ability – or willingness – to draw on the game-experience of the players, to *problematize* it (i.e. present it as a wide-open problem for thought and investigation, as in the Liverpool example above), to let questioning and investigation go wherever they lead, allow adequate time for thought and discussion, and encourage people to link the game-experience with the world of today.

Without an attitude of dialogue, the best teaching aid is still-born. At the staff training conference of an overseas aid charity, one workshop was given a decision-making game on the organization's budget. The task was to cut total expenditure by a defined amount in order to counteract the effects of inflation. Workshop groups could decide priorities and make economies wherever they thought fit – except in overseas aid, which was overwhelmingly the largest single item of expenditure! Since none of the groups questioned this restriction, they not surprisingly produced rather similar recommendations. The manipulation was probably quite unconscious – the workshop organizers took it for granted that the overseas aid programme was inviolable. The effect was to narrow the scope of questioning and angle people's discovery in a desired direction. Dialogue education naturally expresses itself in games, simulation, role play and other participation-techniques, but the dialogue comes from the way they are used, not from the techniques themselves.

A third example comes from Brazil. In the slums of Rio de Janeiro a group of twenty people is at the evening meeting of their cultural circle.[7] They are taking part in a literacy programme worked out by Paulo Freire and his colleagues. In the preceding weeks the adult education team has lived among the people and listened to their conversation, trying to understand both their situation as slum-dwellers and the range and content of their spoken language. Their aim has been to map the cultural and linguistic 'universe' of the people, so as to pick out the constellations of words and ideas which seem most important to them. As a result of this mapping, carried out in dialogue with the people, they have been able to list seventeen significant words. The words all suggest important cultural themes and are in everyday use. They include: *favela* (slum), *chuva* (rain), *terreno* (land), *comida* (food), *bicicleta* (bicycle), *trabalho* (work), *governo* (government), *tijolo* (brick) and *riqueza* (wealth). Since Portuguese is a consistently syllabic language, it is possible to form numerous other words from the syllables in this quite limited list. Thus, from the word ti-jo-lo and its associated syllables (ta-te-ti-to-tu, ja-je-ji-jo-ju etc.) one can make *tatu* (armadillo), *luta* (struggle), *lajota* (flagstone), *jato* (jet) and many others besides.

The researchers have prepared drawings and photographs to go with each of these 'generative words'.[8] These pictures are called 'codifications'. They present some aspect of the people's everyday experience or understanding of life linked always with a particular word. To look at such a picture, describe it, and pose questions about it is to decipher and 'decode' it – to gain mental distance from the daily experience it presents and begin to reflect on it. Tonight, the group is ready to begin learning to read and write. The co-ordinator, a member of the research team, sets up his projector and screen and projects a slide showing the word, *favela*, superimposed on a photograph of the slum area in which the people live. He then starts a problem-posing discussion similar in kind to the Liverpool conversation above. He raises open-ended questions about the favela and its problems – housing, food, clothing, health, education and work. He listens attentively to their comments, lets people talk to each other, and from time to time reformulates the main points made (problematizes them) as new questions for the group.

Next, the word, *favela*, is projected without the picture, and followed immediately by another slide separating it into its syllables: *fa-ve-la*. The group repeats the word and tries to grasp the sounds of its separated syllables. The syllabic 'family' of the first syllable is shown: *fa-fe-fi-fo-fu*. The group members can recognize the syllable, *fa*, which they have already seen, but cannot identify the others. The co-ordinator knows that he must now supply information about the other sounds, but that his fellow-members are knowing subjects capable of thinking for themselves. So he does not immediately name the other sounds, but asks, 'Do these pieces (syllables) have something that makes them alike and something that makes them different?' After a few moments' silence, one of the group says, 'They all begin the same way but they end differently'. 'If they all begin the same way and end differently,' says the co-ordinator, 'can we call them all, *fa*?' 'No', say the members of the group. The co-ordinator then names the other sounds and encourages the group to repeat and learn them. Since the group members themselves have worked out the reason for the differences in sound, the new information is the final piece of a jigsaw they have fitted together themselves rather than a picture fed to them by the co-ordinator.

The co-ordinator then presents the 'families' of the other syllables, one after the other, followed by a slide (aptly called the 'discovery-card') that shows them all together:

$$fa - fe - fi - fo - fu$$
$$va - ve - vi - vo - vu$$
$$la - le - li - lo - lu$$

After a horizontal and vertical reading to strengthen people's grasp of the different sounds, the co-ordinator asks, 'Do you think we can create something with these pieces?' After a silence of perhaps two or three minutes, one of the group members says, falteringly, *'favela'*. *'Favo'*, says another. *'Fivela'*, says a third. Then, rapidly, one after the other, in tones of rising excitement, the group members create the words of their language by combining the syllables before them. On the very first night of the literacy programme in another such cultural circle an illiterate from Brasilia looked at the discovery card of *tijolo* and exclaimed, *'tu ja le* (you already read)!'[9]

The first point to note is that the particular educational aid (projector and slides) is used, not to persuade, entertain, or present people with ideas to absorb, but to help them gain a critical distance from their own everyday life. The fact that such projectors were later denounced as 'subversive' by the Brazilian military government is a tribute to the method rather than their Polish manufacture.

The example also suggests that memorization and repetition still have a part to play in this form of education. At some point it is necessary to receive new data, and to practise, repeat and remember. But the reason for receiving, practising and remembering is that the learners are knowing subjects who want to consolidate their discoveries or gather material for critical inspection, not storage vaults taking someone else's 'facts' on deposit. Wherever possible the co-ordinator of such a group sees and presents the object of knowledge (in this case language, reading and writing) as a problem. Once again, this is not a gimmick to keep the learners happy, but an approach to education arising out of fundamental convictions about the act of knowing, the human being as a knowing subject, and the dialectical relation between the knower and the known.

The co-ordinator's method therefore assumes that these illiterate people at the bottom of the social pyramid already have a culture, express themselves in language, and are capable of using their own words and ideas. They do not need to intone meaningless phrases chosen for them by the authors of literacy textbooks – 'Eva saw the grape', 'The wing is of the bird', 'Mary likes animals', 'If you hammer a nail be careful not to smash your finger'.[10] Indeed, they can from the beginning create their own words and reflect critically on the profound significance of language as an expression of human culture. Experience proves the correctness of these assumptions as well as the effectiveness of the method.

To sum up, dialogue education begins with people's real-life experience. It assumes that their situation (family, school, neighbourhood, work, living conditions, position in society) is the basis of their knowing, and that they already have knowledge, wisdom and culture. It aims to help people gain a critical distance from their experience by reflecting it back to them as an open problem for their investigation. To this end it uses enabling questions which people can respond to out of their experience, and problematizing questions which invite further thought. It accepts the need for some degree of memorization and information-gathering but subordinates both to critical reflection and the needs of the learner. It is based on respect for people, interest in anything they have to contribute, and a belief in their ability to know.

### The teacher and the learner

The above principles drastically alter the relation between the teacher and the learner. The traditional idea of transmission necessarily sees the relationship as unequal. Teacher and learner only achieve equality at the higher levels of education, when both are pressing at the limits of knowledge and exploring a common world.[11] The dialogue model sees teacher and learner as co-equal co-investigators at every stage of learning. Their equality as self-conscious human subjects outweighs the widest differences of age, class and educational standing.

This does not mean that the teacher becomes redundant. Educational leadership remains essential: 'If education is dialogical, it is clear that the role of the teacher is important, whatever the situation.'[12] But the nature of that leadership is altered. It becomes more humble, more easily shared. In any human group – whatever its size – the formal leadership pattern (the appointed 'chairman', 'teacher', 'group leader' etc.) is matched by a different or overlapping informal leadership pattern (every teacher knows who the unofficial leaders are in her class). In dialogue education the teacher carries the leadership baton lightly and is willing to let it pass from hand to hand. She is pleased rather than worried to find another member of the group taking the baton for a few moments and helping everyone to move forward. Given that freedom, the teacher sometimes has the unexpected reward of seeing the shyest and most inarticulate person blossom into speech and command the respect and attention of the rest. I shall never forget the afternoon when the hesitant and unassuming D___ emerged from his six-month silence and transformed the worship group to which I belonged, focusing our thoughts, cutting through tangles, and lifting our whole enterprise to a higher plane.

Dialogue education therefore *unfreezes the roles* of the 'teacher' and the 'learner'. It breaks out of the cramping mould of the transmission model – 'Some teach – others learn; some know – some don't; some transmit – others receive'. Instead, it assumes that all teach and all learn, because all know something and together seek to know more. The opposition between 'teaching' and 'learning' is so entrenched in our language that it is difficult to find terms that do justice to a dialogue relationship. Perhaps the nearest approximation is to speak not of 'teacher' and 'learner' but of the 'teacher-learner' who meets with the 'learner-teachers'. This suggests that the former exercises leadership but expects to learn from the latter, who in turn have the capacity to teach him and learn from each other.[13]

As the examples have shown, the teacher-learner rarely tells and usually questions. He uses enabling questions, not guess-what-I'm-thinking questions. He asks, 'why?', 'how?', 'is this so?', 'is there any connection between what X has said and what Y has said?', 'is there a contradiction here, and if so, why?'. He is suspicious of the single cause and the 'right answer', and thinks instead of reaso*ns*, caus*es*, and meaning*s*. He does not rush to summarize what other people have said or learned, for fear of closing the door to further thought or imposing his own interpretation. He constantly questions his own questions. Do they increase people's will to learn as well as their capacity? Do they increase people's confidence in their ability to know? Do they encourage them to weigh alternatives, look at similarities and contradictions, and classify, reason, or decide? Do they generate new questions of which the hearers were previously unaware?[14]

The teacher-learner can put questions in this way because she has never stopped questioning what she herself knows. She has questioning in her bones. However many times she has previously considered it, a particular object of knowledge is still a problem and a mystery. If this sounds startling, think of the best teachers you have known, and ask whether they did not have something of excitement and exploration – the ability to introduce a theory, a problem or a work of art as if they were discovering it for the first time. In dialogue education the teacher-learner is able to *re-live* her acts of knowing a hundred times over, to 're-cognize' her previous cognitions. There is not for her one moment when she knows, discovers and solves problems (in the silence of the study) and another, different moment (in the noise of the classroom) when she tells and transmits both problem and solution. She does not know 'x' and then pass it on unchanged to A, then later to B, then later to C. Instead, she tests her knowledge of 'x' with A, modifies it from A's act of knowing, and modifies it again with B and C.

Again, it is a contradiction in terms not to be gripped by something one is presenting to others as a problem. If I am leading a group in the Village Enclosure game, and asking them to weigh the pros and cons of enclosure from the viewpoint of the squire, rector, yeomen and freeholders, I cannot present the question problematically unless I myself experience its problematic nature. I cannot say, 'This is a problem for you but not for me, because I know the answer' – for that would reduce the problem to a puzzle by asking the others to guess the 'answer' that I was trying to transmit to them. Nor can I say, 'This is a problem for you but not for me because I have worked through it before and am bored with it' – for if so, I would be denying its relevance and the boredom would show itself in my presentation. In both cases I would cease to be in dialogue by elevating myself above the other members of the group. It is psychologically impossible to present something to people as a problem and stay detached from it, as a mere spectator.[15]

The teacher-learner measures the effectiveness of his approach, not by the amount of information that the learner-teachers remember, but by changes in their ability to question, reason, and think critically about what they know. He will expect them to show more confidence in their ability to learn, rely more on their own judgment yet be ready to modify their first opinion, have more respect for evidence and logical argument, and be more cautious and provisional in answering a question, yet ready to test out their conclusions by action.

'Dialogue' in this kind of education is not 'A depositing facts in B', nor 'A and B depositing facts in each other', nor a polemic where each one seeks to overpower the other. It is a listening relationship where people respect each other as much as they question each other, and vice-versa. It is founded on human and Christian values. 'Dialogue cannot exist . . . in the absence of a profound love for the world and for men . . . Love is at the same time the foundation of dialogue and dialogue itself.'[16] Dialogue is only possible if the teacher-learner and the learner-teachers have an attitude of humility and respect. 'How can I enter into a dialogue if I always project ignorance onto others and never perceive my own?'[17] Dialogue depends on mutual trust and cannot exist if one party's words do not coincide with his or her actions. Finally, dialogue springs from a profound faith in people – in their potential to know, discover, create, and give something significant to the world and to each other.[18]

Faith in people is a self-fulfilling prophecy. The transmission model of education almost inevitably assumes that the 'learners' do not know, or know very little, or that what they know has no relevance to the matter in hand. Such an attitude reinforces people's natural shyness or hesitation, and blinds the transmitting educator to their knowledge or potential. Teachers who want to plant knowledge in supposedly ignorant children are likely both to devalue the child's culture and betray their own ignorance. Thus, children in Tuscany found with surprise that their teachers couldn't tell cherry trees from plum trees, didn't know the varied uses of vine-shoots, and used textbooks with laughably inaccurate illustrations of rural life.[19]

By contrast, the dialogue approach is more likely to call forth such knowledge, because it assumes that the learner-teachers already know much of value, that what they know is relevant, and that they have the potential for critical thought. On the *fifth day* of the literacy programme described above, a previously illiterate member of a Rio Grande do Norte cultural circle went to the blackboard to write, as he called it, a 'thinking word' – '"*o povo vai resouver os poblemos do Brasil votando conciente*" ("the people will solve the problems of Brazil by informed voting")'.[20]

An even more striking example comes from a cultural circle in Santiago. The co-ordinator showed a picture of a drunken man walking along the street and three young men lounging at the corner. 'What do you see?', he asked. 'What is happening here?' 'The only one there who is productive and useful to his country,' came the reply, 'is the souse who is returning home after working all day for low wages and who is worried about his family because he can't take care of their needs ... *He is a decent worker, and a souse like us.*'[21] Such an honest identification with the drunkard – 'a souse like us' – suggests a considerable degree of trust between the co-ordinator and the group members. It also shows up an attitude and interpretation of slum life that would not easily occur to anyone looking at it from outside. It points to a possible connection between earning low wages, feeling exploited, worrying about one's family, and getting drunk. It therefore opens up many important themes for investigation.

Few transmitting educators could be aware of such attitudes in advance, or be able to probe further into them. By definition, a transmitting educator would come to the people with some message or 'knowledge' to impart – most likely on the addictive pattern of alcoholism. He would probably see the sobriety of the young men as socially desirable or as a moral virtue. To present this view as 'knowledge' would either prevent the listener's viewpoint from emerging, or devalue it if it emerged. Problem-posing dialogue can bring out what one-way education would suppress, devalue, or never discover.

## Some common objections

To change from transmission to dialogue takes time, effort – and courage. It may therefore be helpful to look at some of the more obvious objections.

1. *It's ridiculous to say that the learner is the source of knowledge. That simply means pooling our ignorance.*
    Education begins with the experience and real-life situation of the people taking part. This does not mean that it should end there. A thoughtful educator would hope to build on the Liverpool girls' understanding of free will by encouraging them to apply it more widely. The generative words used by the cultural circle in Rio de Janeiro have considerable possibilities of extension beyond the concrete and everyday. 'Land' suggests an investigation of the *latifundium*[22] and its history, and of land ownership, natural resources, and food production. 'Work' could suggest an enquiry into wages, inflation, and the relation between capital, management and labour. 'Government' and 'wealth' are equally open to further exploration. The objection also underestimates the capacity of quite ordinary groups of people to produce new knowledge.

2. *It is unnecessary to expect people to re-discover for themselves all the knowledge already gained in the past.*
    The wheel has long been invented. A child does not re-invent it. He can however be allowed the freedom to discover and explore its uses, not have such 'knowledge' planted in him. Dialogue education does not expect people to forget all that the human race has gained, and start from scratch to create it again. It insists that what has been achieved, the world of culture that has already shaped us, needs to be discovered and critically investigated by each human subject. As the history game suggests, 'everything can be presented problematically.'[23]

3. *We can't afford to waste time letting people discover in two hours what they could be told in ten minutes.*

The objector is probably looking at the use of time from the viewpoint of the teacher. This is not necessarily identical with the viewpoint of the learners. If I give a lecture lasting twenty minutes, it can encompass ideas and analysis that it would take perhaps three or four hours to present problematically (e.g. in role play, pictures, group work, discussion). The lecture may be coherent, clear and interesting – to me. Unfortunately, this is no guarantee that it will be equally useful to everyone else. All the audience will have done after twenty minutes is to listen, and perhaps take notes. This is of doubtful value even in terms of retaining what has been said.[24] To weigh it, question it, gain critical distance from it, and take the thinking and investigation *where the listeners want it to go* would take considerably longer than the delivery time, and could not be achieved in terms of a transmission approach to education. The objector assumes that 'letting people discover' is a procedure which does not include the educator, that people should only discover what the educator wants to present to them, and that in any case, 'telling them' is all that is required. On closer inspection the objector is simply stating a preference for the transmission model.

4. *If I don't keep a grip on the meeting/class/discussion it might go completely off the track.*

Behind such objections is a fear of 'losing control'. If the educator has always regarded himself – and has been regarded – as the authority, the one who knows, whose duty it is to tell others and direct the business of education, it is hard to make such a radical change of roles. Change can only grow out of a conviction that dialogue and its methods are strongly to be preferred, accompanied by a re-casting of the image that the teacher has of himself, and a serious attempt to develop a new leadership style. From experience I can only say that the change is entirely beneficial. To drop the artificial burden of being a licensed knowall is as liberating as the discovery that other people do not need to be 'controlled', that chaos does not result if their questioning goes where it wills, and that the learner-teachers can give as much to the teacher-learner as he or she to them. The teacher-learner becomes free to be an *educator*, perhaps for the first time.

5. *All this is nothing new.*

It is true that new ideas are often in part a re-shaping of what has gone before. There is no shame in admitting that wisps and strands of dialogue education have been floating in the air for some time, or that Socrates also used a questioning method. It is more important to note what its consequences were for Socrates, and to ask whether the new developments are valid and relevant. If they are, the debate over their degree of novelty can be left to the angels and the academics. No doubt there were people in Gutenberg's time who said that of course his new technique of printing was only a more elaborate way of making playing cards.

## A clash of models

Beneath the clash between 'transmission' and 'dialogue' there is at least one point of agreement. Both points of view use the word 'education' to mean deliberate attempts to organize learning. Thus, a working definition of dialogue education would be *the intentional creation of situations in which people can make acts of knowing, characterized by an atmosphere of dialogue and a problem-posing use of educational aids and techniques, and with the aim of developing a critical consciousness.*

The transmission model of education has three positive elements. Firstly, it recognizes that memorization and information-gathering are necessary parts of education. Yet it also exaggerates their importance. It suggests that mental recall is the highest form of intellectual achievement and that the collection of unrelated facts is the goal of education. The persistence of recall and memorization as goals of education may be, in part, a cultural jet-lag from the age before the jet. In earlier societies, knowledge changed slowly. Traditional wisdom was the result of countless ages of trial and error, and the new generation could not risk its survival by trifling with it. To remember and apply it was therefore of vital importance. In the last two hundred years, however, knowledge has been increasingly based on experiment and the rate of social change has accelerated. The ability to remember and recall information has therefore become almost irrelevant. If – *if* – you remember what you were taught at school, you are almost certainly a walking encyclopaedia of outdated information.[25]

A dialogue approach to education therefore sees information gathering and memorization as the servants of critical awareness and perceived relevance. In a working class area of Coventry, local people who initially came to seek help at an Advice and Information Centre joined its staff and acquired considerable skill in dealing with welfare rights applications.[26] In an Educational Priority Area of Liverpool, over seven hundred council tenants (out of a population of six thousand) listened attentively to a detailed explanation of the 1972 Housing Finance Act, and many were able to act on their knowledge.[27] In the United States, the community development movement in the 1960s helped to stimulate the emergence of an articulate, informed and militant leadership in the most 'deprived' and 'apathetic' areas of the big cities.[28] There is ample evidence that most people can grasp and memorize detailed information on issues which directly concern them. *On a dialogue understanding of education, 'information' is what people want to know or know they need to know – not what someone else thinks they ought to know.*

A second important element in the transmission model is its assumption that educational communication is bound up with a personal relationship. The teachers whose memory we most prize influenced us as much by their personalities as by the 'subject' they taught. The weakness of the transmission model is that it freezes the roles of teacher and learner. It exaggerates the 'knowledge' of the former and the 'ignorance' of the latter. It confuses the authority of truth and insight with the prestige of the teacher, and he or she becomes the person who is paid to know.

Finally, the traditionalist's urge to 'transmit' or 'initiate' expresses, at its best, a longing to generate excitement in others about the things one believes in or has discovered to be of value. The architect of 'education as initiation', R. S. Peters, points out that conditioning is not education and that to say this implies that conditioning is bad. We refuse to equate the two because conditioning implies the creation of responses in people without their knowledge or consent, whereas education should be freely and knowingly entered into. 'To say that we are educating people commits us, in other words, to morally legitimate procedures.'[29]

On this view, education means 'the transmission of knowledge and skills deemed to be worthwhile, in ways deemed to be proper'.[30]

The crucial question is, *who decides what is thought to be worthwhile?* Is it the teacher, the people being educated, or the educational system as an expression of social and economic values –such as thrift or co-operation, capitalism or socialism? R. S. Peters recognizes that it is most likely to be the education system. When people speak of education, he argues, one must ask what their standards of value are. When talking of the education system of a community, 'we need not think that what is going on is worth-while, but members of the society, whose system it is, must think it is'.[31]

On this point, the two opposing models of education converge in unexpected agreement. The theory and practice of any form of education has certain built-in values, be they religious, moral or political. No one can therefore avoid the question, 'which values?' *There is no such thing as a neutral education that simply 'tells people the facts'.*

# 3

## Justice in Rational Thought

Half had breakfast, half had none –
Some had too much dinner, but the rest have not begun.
Half have got no clothes to wear –
What do you think of that? *It's not fair!*

John Bailey[1]

For Justice, though she's painted blind
is to the weaker side inclined.

Samuel Butler, *Hudibras*

People's feelings about social justice do not always match their social position. Between 1918 and 1960, working class[2] militancy in Britain waxed and waned with war, boom and slump. It did not correspond at all closely with actual inequalities of wealth. After the Second World War, the middle classes frequently felt aggrieved at losing ground to manual workers, though their sense of grievance was stronger than the facts appear to warrant.[3]

Historical evidence on the gap between facts and feelings was confirmed by a social survey carried out in 1961. One question asked was, 'Do you think that there are any other sorts of people doing noticeably better at the moment than you or your family?' Those who answered 'Yes' were asked, 'What sort of people?' and what they felt about it. Though our society showed marked inequalities of income, *over a quarter* of working class people, including some of the very poorest, could not think of any people who were noticeably better off than themselves. Awareness of people being better off was higher in the middle classes than in the working class.

Moreover, when asked what sorts of people were noticeably

better off, few of those interviewed spread their comparisons very wide. 'People with no children', said a mother of four. 'People who get extra money by letting off part of the house', said an eighty-two year old widow. 'Army officers who retired since I did', said a retired army officer. 'People farming in a bigger way who can get subsidies', said a smallholder not entitled to any. 'University research people who went into research instead of teaching', said a schoolmaster's wife. Given the facts of income distribution, one might have expected people to compare themselves with business executives or high-earning professionals. Yet most people thought only in terms of those closest to them on the social scale.[4]

To say that people's sense of injustice can be higher or lower than the facts apparently warrant suggests that there is some standard of independent judgment. It implies a conception of what people *ought* to feel. If inequalities of wealth and status are inevitable or even desirable, then people in a lower position ought to be content with it and 'know their place'. On the other hand, if some inequalities are not inevitable, and gross inequalities are abhorrent, then people ought to feel a sense of injustice about them. It then becomes right to educate for justice by increasing people's knowledge of inequalities, widening their range of comparison, and creating a critical consciousness that turns grievance or guilt into action.

Thus, whoever talks about injustice in society, or claims that inequality is not as unjust as it appears to be, has some ideal standard of social justice which he or she is using as a target or reference point. Disagreements about how unjust our society actually is do not merely stem from different estimates of what is changeable and what is inevitable. They also reflect different convictions about what is just and what is unjust, what makes a situation *unjust* rather than simply unpleasant or unbearable, and what sorts of inequality are morally defensible if inequality is defensible at all.

An ideal standard is just that – ideal. It will seem 'impossible' and 'unrealistic' to anyone who does not share it, who despairs of change, or who is content with things as they are. Yet it is important to have a clear understanding of what the ideal is – whether or not it seems attainable. By itself, the clearest ideal of social justice is powerless and inert. When added to the belief that change is possible, it gives vision, depth and energy to our action.

## Basic ideas of justice

The basic idea of justice is giving people their due, what they deserve or ought to have. To work out what is due to people demands thought and calculation, especially if the people concerned are not known to us personally, but are classes and groups in society. Justice is therefore rational rather than impulsive or emotional. Rational thinking is marked by consistency. It does not change its mind haphazardly, according to whim or prejudice. If it decides that the age of eighteen is sufficiently adult for a male or female person of British nationality to have the vote, it will not give the vote to someone under eighteen, or deny it to any eighteen-year-old who fulfils these conditions.

Consistency demands that what is due to one person who is a British national of eighteen years and over is equally due to any other person who has the same characteristics. 'Justice cannot be applied except between people who have some relevant attribute in common'[5] and, to be consistent, it must give them equal treatment.

It would be easy to jump from this to the conclusion that justice therefore means giving equal treatment to everyone. But this would be too long a jump from the simple idea of consistency. *It can only be made if one also believes that people have so much in common because they are human beings that – whatever their differences – justice requires equal treatment for all.* A theory of social justice must either take such fundamental equality for granted, give reasons for rejecting it, or explain what human beings have in common that requires it. Since people are obviously not equal in every respect, a theory of social justice must also say which inequalities really matter, and how far different sorts of inequality are justified.[6]

The idea of equality expands the idea of consistency and fuses with it to give four principles which apply to the traditional understanding of justice in Western societies.

The first principle is *generality*. When a man called Harry Bridges was being tried in the American courts, a senator stated that if the Supreme Court did not decide against Bridges he intended to introduce a 'law' that would single him out for deportation. Such a law would not be just – and would not in the United

States be lawful – even if everyone voted for it including Harry Bridges himself. A law can lay down conditions for deportation of a general kind – 'anyone who does x shall be liable to deportation'. It cannot in justice go from the general to the particular. It cannot single out particular individuals, or make particular exceptions. Generality therefore also implies universality. Just laws apply to all. Lawmakers and legislators are not exempt from obedience to the laws they make. Justice decrees that 'every one who favours a measure shall run the risk of being the one disfavoured by its terms'.[7]

Justice also means *impartiality* – equal treatment before the law. 'You shall not pervert justice, either by favouring the poor or by subservience to the great', says the book of Leviticus, reflecting a legal tradition already many hundreds of years old.[8] Justice must also be *predictable in its working*, so that everyone can see its consistency. 'The Rule of Law stands for the view that decisions should be made by the application of known principles or laws. In general such decisions will be predictable, and the citizen will know where he is'.[9]

Finally, our tradition of social justice has become linked with the idea of democracy, or equal participation in government. Many of our current political issues – urban redevelopment, Welsh and Scottish nationalism, regional devolution, and the conflict in Northern Ireland – are centred round the problem of whether existing political frameworks can give fair and effective participation.

### *'Justice as fairness'*

The above notions are tied together coherently in a modern theory of 'justice as fairness', developed by John Rawls.[10] The basic question he sets out to answer is, '*What principles of social justice would free and rational persons accept if they chose such principles in a situation of genuine equality* (that is, without the vested interests of class, race, social position etc. which normally bias our thinking)?' The greatest difficulty in answering this question is to understand clearly what such a situation of equality would mean. Rawls calls it the 'original position'. For simplicity I shall cast it in the form of a fable, hoping to avoid serious distortion.[11]

Suppose that it is the year 3136. A starship is on its way from earth to colonize a distant planet. Despite advances in astrophysics and space technology, the journey will take several generations of earth time. To prevent ageing, the passengers are sealed in separate cocoons, and kept in a kind of suspended animation. After the launching and acceleration period they have a normal rhythm of waking and sleeping, and are fully conscious during the waking periods, being able to think, hear, see and speak. At the beginning of the first waking period, they emerge from unconsciousness in a state of amnesia. Each person looks round his small cocoon, registers the fact that his mind is a complete blank, yet feels no anxiety, nor any other emotion beyond a mild surprise and curiosity. As the passengers wake, the following briefing appears on a screen in front of them:

You are one of a thousand human beings on board the starship E-3136-I, travelling from earth to colonize a distant planet. You are in a condition of space-hibernation and your full personality will be restored at the end of your journey.

Meanwhile, you will find yourself in total ignorance of your name, your sex, your age, or your natural assets and abilities. You will have no knowledge of your level of intelligence, your physical skills, or your artistic or scientific capability. You have no access to your religious or moral convictions, and do not know whether your attitude towards them is one of doubt, acceptance or strong conviction. You do not know whether you are extrovert or introvert, cautious or willing to take risks, optimistic or pessimistic about life. You have no means of estimating your past or future place in society, and have no memory of your income, status, or degree of power and influence.

Under this veil of ignorance,[12] you and your fellow-passengers must agree on the basic principles that will govern your new society. In trying to reach agreement, each person's opinion carries equal weight, and each one of you has an equal say.

In your condition of space hibernation, it is impossible for you to communicate directly with other passengers. The ship's computer will collate and store opinions, and inform you of any suggestions that others have made. When everyone has reached agreement, the computer will announce the result. The eventual decision will therefore be unanimous.

Each one of you has a rational aim in life, a plan for your own fulfilment. At present, you do not know anything about yourself, so cannot say what your particular plan of life is. But you will want the freedom, the means and the opportunity to fulfil your rational aims, whatever they turn out to be.

Each of your fellow-passengers also has a rational plan of life which is valid and worthwhile to them. Some people's aims will be close enough to make co-operation possible. Others will clash with yours to a greater or lesser extent. You will therefore need principles which can regulate your different claims in the fairest and most rational way. Your new society will therefore be a co-operative venture. Each of its members will be closely linked with the others, while each seeks his or her own fulfilment.

You each have a reasonable degree of intelligence, and a normal ability to keep agreements and act on the promises you have made. You have enough information about the general laws of human nature and society to make a realistic decision.

Your new planet will provide sufficient though modest resources for your society's material needs. It will be necessary to colonize it as rapidly as possible. Accordingly, the starship's embryo-banks already contain your unborn children. You will arrive in your new society as the head of a family. You must therefore consider the welfare of the next generation as well as your own.

Your agreement will be public, general, and universal. Since all must agree to it, it is binding on all. It cannot be renegotiated once the veil of ignorance has been removed.

Please begin your work now.

### The stages of reasoning

Faced with such a task and situation, the passengers would quickly realize that in their cocoons of ignorance no one can unduly influence the others by sheer force of personality. Because they know nothing of their talents or social position, they cannot reach agreement by bargaining with each other. They cannot give up some advantages in return for others, because they have literally nothing to bargain with. They cannot debate with each other or form coalitions and majorities. Oratory, prestige, charm, wealth, power, and all the other normal accompaniments of our reasoning skills, are absent. They have to make a social contract[13] based on reason, and arrived at by rational argument.

One consequence of this is that, since no one knows what their natural characteristics are, and everyone knows that the contract will be final and binding, irrational suggestions like discrimination based on sex, height, size of feet, date of birth or skin colour will be quickly rejected.

The passengers will also realize that they cannot ignore each other. Their society is to be a co-operative venture. If I am one such passenger, I can only gain the best possible chance for my own rational aims, whatever they turn out to be, if I take other people's likely aims into account. I shall need to look for principles which allow for the greatest possible variety of rational aims, both for my own benefit and for the good of others. In my cocoon of ignorance I can be neither an egotist nor an altruist. For since I do not yet know what my aims and hopes are, I can neither pursue them at the expense of others nor give them up for others' benefit.

From their general understanding of psychology, the passengers know that to follow their aim in life with vigour and delight they will need a basic confidence in their own worth as persons, a sense of self-respect. Self-respect depends to a considerable degree on the respect of others. Unless someone else values and upholds the worthwhileness of my aims, it will be extremely difficult for me to carry on believing that they are worthwhile. The passengers will probably therefore agree that the principles they draw up must be based on mutual respect. It is in their rational self-interest to have a society which shows respect for the dignity and worth of each individual person.

While the passengers each have a normal ability to keep agreements and act on their principles, they also know that their agreement will be final and binding. So they will want to avoid making an agreement which might demand too much of them. If I am among the passengers, I shall want an agreement which I can reasonably expect to honour in the worst possible circumstances. The society I help to build must be capable of inspiring the willing co-operation of all its members, including the poorest, weakest, and least naturally gifted – who might well include myself.

Thus, if I am a passenger on that starship, my reasoning will almost certainly lead me to one conclusion: *Whatever else I agree to about our new society I must make sure that I could accept being one of its weakest or least fortunate members.* At present, I know nothing about my natural gifts, my social position, or even whether I am the sort of person who is cautious or likes taking risks. I do know that many of the aims of the other passengers will conflict with mine, and that their attitudes towards me will vary considerably. I might end up in a position where I am receiving orders from people who dislike me, where I belong to a small minority, or where I have few natural gifts. If I do find myself in such a position, I shall want to be sure that my freedom to develop, my enjoyment of life, and my share in the benefits of society, have all been safeguarded.

Moreover, since I am the head of a family, I have a responsibility to the next generation. Even if I knew that I had the moral strength to sacrifice my own self-interest (and I don't know this) I could not sacrifice the chances of others. Nor can I take risks with their chances or my own. I must protect myself against the worst possibility rather than gamble on the best.

### *The first principle – equal liberty*

The passengers have sufficient general knowledge to distinguish natural benefits from social benefits.[14] Natural benefits are individual talents and abilities such as height, physical strength, physical skills, artistic and scientific gifts. They are mainly a matter of individual heredity and are only indirectly influenced by the organization of society. Social benefits come directly from the way a society is organized. They include civil rights, civil liberties, and varying degrees of wealth, income, power and status.

Whatever else the passengers may need to fulfil their as yet unknown aims in life, they can be reasonably sure that they will need as many of the social benefits as possible, and as much of each as possible. Whatever my aim in life turns out to be, it will be difficult to pursue it if I have no freedom of thought, speech or movement, or if I have no share at all in the wealth that my society produces. Since I do not yet know what my aim in life is, I cannot assume that I will be willing to accept less than the highest possible level of social benefits – though when it comes to the point I would be free to refrain from using them. My fellow passengers can reasonably be expected to have a similar attitude. We shall therefore need to find a principle which gives each of us as many social benefits as possible without depriving anyone else.

Social benefits can be divided into two groups. First, there are the basic liberties of citizenship which can be guaranteed by law. They include freedom of speech, assembly and conscience, freedom of movement and residence, freedom from arbitrary arrest, and the freedom and duty to share fully in government. Given the chain of reasoning above, the passengers on the starship will almost certainly agree that *each person is to have an equal right to the most extensive basic liberties compatible with a like liberty for all.* This principle implies order as well as freedom. In a decision-making assembly, for example, all have the right to speak, but not to speak all at once. Limits are placed on freedom in order to make everyone equally free.

### *The second principle – social and economic sharing*

The other group of social benefits consists of various social and economic advantages. Some are created by the way a society produces its material goods, and the resulting distribution of income and wealth. Others arise from the need for leadership and authority, which give some people the right to issue orders and make decisions, and so enjoy more power than others. Three general principles apply to them both.

Firstly, the passengers have already agreed that the structure of their society must demonstrate a respect for the dignity and worth of every single one of its members. It is not enough to think of the average satisfaction of the whole, or the average well-being of different groups. Their agreement must not ask too much of anyone, and must command the willing assent of those who turn out to be the poorer, weaker and least naturally gifted members of their society. This means that any inequality of power, status or wealth must be rationally justified, and accepted as just, by its weakest and poorest members.

Similarly, in deciding on their basic principles the passengers are trying to safeguard their own position if they turn out to be among the least advantaged members of their society. It follows that any inequalities must be seen and judged from the standpoint of the least advantaged, not from the average, majority or better-off point of view.

Finally, the starship passengers have to deal with the fact that natural benefits are certain to be unequally distributed. In the best possible society some people will be more gifted, more intelligent, more pleasing in appearance, or more resourceful than others. Since the passengers know that they might end up with few if any such advantages, they will hardly decide to let the most gifted have free rein to capitalize on their gifts. On the other hand, they will not want to suppress or eradicate such differences – for their new society will need all the leadership, talent and ability it can produce. It follows that they will decide to regard all natural benefits – from physical strength to musical genius – as a common asset, to be used for the good of all, and especially for the good of the least favoured. Accordingly, they are likely to agree that social and economic inequalities shall be arranged so that they are to the greatest benefit of the least advantaged members of society.

All societies have differences in power and authority. For the sake of order and efficiency the starship passengers will probably agree that some people must have authority over others, and that decision-making needs to be focused in particular people or groups. Yet they have also agreed that everyone has certain freedoms which no power or authority can override. Moreover, it is unlikely that inequalities of power and authority can be to the greatest benefit of the least advantaged, or secure their willing co-operation, unless they have some control over those who exercise such power. People who give orders must therefore be answerable to those who receive them.

The new society will not be static. It will develop from generation to generation. Without a continuing effort, natural and social inequalities will almost certainly multiply, so that the children of people with power, wealth or natural gifts enjoy an unfair advantage over others. Thus, it is not enough to guarantee formal 'equality of opportunity' by making positions of authority legally open to all. The new society will also need to create a *fair* equality of opportunity – by positive discrimination in favour of the least advantaged, so that legal equality has real meaning. This implies a continuing redistribution of wealth and power in favour of the poorest members of society.

Taking the above points together, the starship passengers will probably agree that *inequalities of wealth, power, status and income in their new society can only be justified if they are to the greatest benefit of the least advantaged, and if they go with positions or appointments which are open to all under conditions of fair equality of opportunity*. This principle implies that natural talents and gifts should be treated as a common asset and that people who give orders should be answerable to those who receive them.[15]

### Comments and criticisms

A basic assumption of justice as fairness is that each of the individuals in a society is entitled to equal respect as a human being.[16] The strength of John Rawls' theory is that, starting from this basic conviction, he tries to work out principles of justice based solely on reason. The original position of equality, represented here by the starship, is a metaphor which can help us to separate reasoning about justice from the vested interests of class, culture and personal temperament which normally bias our thinking.

Yet the same basic assumption is also a source of weakness. By definition, the people in the original position are separate individuals. Each is a self-contained unit, completely unaffected by the others. In fact, however, no human being can exist in this isolated way. We know ourselves only in relationships. What we are as individuals is fundamentally shaped by our membership of groups, such as our family, social class, nation or race. To picture society as made up of self-contained individuals who make a contract with each other is to ignore the fundamental importance of the groups and classes to which those individuals belong.

On Rawls' own theory the people in the original position would have a general knowledge of society and history. They would therefore have some understanding of the importance of group membership. Part of their general knowledge would surely be that some societies show deep clashes of interest between different social groups – between rulers and ruled or rich and poor for example. Even though they do not know what their own point of view about such clashes will be, they will have to admit the possibility that some clashes between groups or classes in their new society might be irreconcilable, and that members of the best-off groups might not willingly surrender their privileges for the benefit of the least-advantaged as the second principle of justice as fairness requires.

Thus, if I am a passenger on the starship I have to take account of the possibility that I am a member of the best-off class in a society scarred by deep social conflict, and unwilling to surrender my privileges except under duress. Once I admit this as even a slight possibility, a social contract becomes impossible – for I also know that I must avoid making any agreement which I might find it impossible to keep.[17]

Rawls' reasoning for the two principles of justice only stands up, then, if we think of people as self-contained individuals, each pursuing their own path in a society with little or no social conflict.[18] Since this is a one-sided view of human nature and society, the theory can only have partial validity. If there is enough truth in the belief that every individual is of equal worth to make it part of our ideal of social justice, Rawls' two principles can be accepted as a starting point. But they will need to be balanced by an understanding of the real world, where group and class memberships are as important as individual aims, and where social conflict is an inescapable part of social life.

Even as a starting point, however, the theory of justice as fairness is a challenging standard for our own society. It shows that, for anyone who takes equality of worth seriously, a society must be judged from the standpoint of its weakest and poorest members. 'The test of inequalities is whether they can be justified to the losers; and for the winners to be able to do this, they must be prepared, in principle, to change places.'[19] By this test, our world and society are markedly unjust. The two principles also suggest that *all comparisons are legitimate*. On the evidence, people in British society do not make their range of comparison as wide as they are in justice entitled to do. There is no reason, on Rawls' two principles, why an assembly-line worker in a car factory should not compare his income and status with that of judges, accountants and company chairmen as well as with boilermakers, railwaymen and fellow factory-workers.

# 4

# Justice in Christian Faith

Any justice which is only justice soon degenerates into something less than justice. It must be saved by something which is more than justice.

Reinhold Niebuhr[1]

Christian thinking about social justice has three distinct though intertwining strands. The first goes back to the early Christian Fathers and has been particularly developed in Roman Catholic teaching. It believes that there is a *natural justice* called for by our very existence as human beings on this planet. Because God creates humanity in his own image and likeness, he gives to every single person a unique yet equal value and dignity. Beneath our natural differences there is an equality of worth which outweighs them all.

Natural justice is expressed in three basic principles. Firstly, because each person has a God-given dignity and worth, every social system and structure should have the needs of the human person as its central aim and its sole reason for existence.[2] Equal dignity and worth imply, secondly, that all the earth's resources, goods and gifts should be fairly shared, not divided on the basis of finder's keepers, political power, or accidents of geography. 'God intended the earth and all that it contains for the use of every human being and people.'[3] Finally, justice means promoting the common good of humanity – not the greatest good of the greatest number, nor merely a reasonable material standard of living, but the conditions of life which will allow each person, family and group to find its highest possible fulfilment.[4] The goal of economic development, therefore, is not quantity but quality. The purpose of production is not the mere multiplication of products. 'It must not be profit or domination. Rather, it must be the service of man, and indeed of the whole man.'[5]

The equal worth of all human beings in a modern interdependent world demands fundamental changes in the name of natural justice. From early times, Christian faith has held that 'those things which some possess in excess of reasonable needs are owed by natural law to the sustenance of the poor'.[6] Previous definitions of reasonable needs allowed people to claim that, given the present order of society, the wants of their particular social class were reasonable. Pope John proposed a more radical definition: 'The obligation of everyman', he said, 'the urgent obligation of the Christian, is to reckon what is superfluous by the measure of the needs of others.'[7] He also drew the conclusion that justice implies redistribution: 'The economic wealth of a people arises not only from an aggregate abundance of goods but also, and more so, from their *real and efficacious redistribution according to justice*, as a guarantee of the personal development of the members of society.'[8]

Because God creates and loves all human beings everywhere, the fundamental human unit is not the nation state but the world community. Christian faith has therefore been quick to see that the problems of pollution and limits to growth are essentially problems of justice. Until quite recently, it was assumed that there were no limits to our capacity to raise standards of living by gaining control over nature. Justice therefore meant giving the poor some say in present decisions and some hope of future gain. As the cake grew larger, everyone's slice would get bigger, no matter how small their share. Today 'we face each other once again with the stark realisation that in a finite world one man's wealth is another man's poverty.'[9] 'We are linked together by the urgent need to preserve our precious resources of air and water, of land and minerals. We must be good stewards of the whole earth for ourselves and our descendants.'[10]

Perhaps the most challenging feature of this tradition is its attitude to ownership. If goods and gifts are meant to serve the common good they must be treated as a common asset, not subject to a free-for-all. 'Man ought to possess external things not as his own, but as common, in such a way ... that he is ready to communicate them to others in need.'[11] Our 'ownership' of anything – house, car, manual skills or mental agility – is not freehold, but leasehold. It is a privilege, not an absolute right. The fair division of goods and gifts has first priority. It overrides all other rights of ownership, business, and trade.[12] If a person is in extreme necessity, he even has the right to take from the riches of others what he himself needs.[13]

## Saving justice

The second strand of Christian thinking about justice is drawn from the story of a religious experience. It is the common heritage of Christians and Jews.

In this story, the Hebrew people first know their God as the God who sets them free from slavery and oppression. The exodus from Egypt is not just one among many of their traditions. It is the foundation of their knowledge of God and their existence as a nation. The kernel of the story is that Israel was an oppressed people, enslaved in Pharaoh's Egypt. Against all the odds they gained their freedom under the leadership of Moses, and were allowed to leave. At some point on their journey, at the 'sea of reeds',[14] this defenceless people faced the overwhelming force of Pharaoh's army. By events now obscure to us, they found themselves wonderfully delivered, through no power of their own. These events convinced them that Yahweh, the God they had long worshipped, was powerful beyond measure, and utterly to be trusted.

By itself, this experience would not have distinguished Israel from other tribes, and Yahweh from other gods. But Yahweh – a God of nomads, not a fertility spirit of the fields – has a character unlike any other God. He is not only mighty, awesome and holy. He is also *righteous*. His love is fierce and demanding. He has a passion for truth and justice.

Israel's fundamental experience, then is of *the righteous God who sets his people free*, not because they are mighty or worthy, but because he loves them and chooses them as his own.[15]

The liberation from Egypt is more than a merely 'political' event. But neither is it purely 'religious' or 'spiritual'. It delivers the people from economic and political oppression, but calls them to give themselves totally to Yahweh. This calling is embodied in a solemn Covenant at Mount Sinai. By this Covenant Yahweh makes Israel his holy people, promises his continuing love, and gives them his law. The people of Israel answer his call and bind themselves to reflect his righteousness in their national life:

> For the Lord your God is God of gods and Lord of lords, the great, mighty and terrible God. He is no respecter of persons, and is not to be bribed; he secures justice for widows and orphans, and loves the alien who lives among you, giving him food and clothing. You too must love the alien, for you once lived as aliens in Egypt.[16]

The reference to the immigrant alien is echoed many times in the detailed laws of Exodus and Leviticus. Some of these laws concern rituals and customs that are strange to us. Others reflect a common Near Eastern tradition of public law going back to Hammurabi. But some, including the law of the alien, are peculiar to Israel, and reflect Israel's experience of God. The members of the Covenant people are to show Yahweh's kind of justice to each other. They are not to ill-treat any widow or fatherless child, for Yahweh has sworn to defend them. The universal Near Eastern practice of charging interest on a loan is forbidden if the borrower is a poor man. If an Israelite takes his neighbour's cloak in pawn, he must restore it by sunset, because it is the debtor's only clothing.[17] When he reaps his wheat crop or gathers in the grapes, he is to leave the gleanings for the poor and the alien. When he hires a day labourer he must pay him at sunset, not hold back his wages till next morning. He must not treat the deaf with contempt nor put an obstacle in the way of the blind. He must not seek revenge nor cherish anger against his kinsfolk, but must love his neighbour as a man like himself.[18]

This understanding of justice is intuitive rather than rational. Yet neither is it *irrational*. The religious conviction can be elaborated in laws marked by consistency, predictability and generality. Perhaps it is best described as a *trans-rational* understanding of justice, as reason fired by passion, as faith worked out in rational forms. The Hebrew poets could without difficulty picture the Messiah wearing justice as a belt and righteousness as a girdle. They could speak of God raining down justice from the skies and making it blossom on earth, of justice rolling on like a river and of justice and peace holding hands.[19] The ideal citizen is the righteous man, whose practical action for justice shows

that he truly knows God,[20] and who pursues justice with zest and
delight:

> The man threatened with ruin blessed me,
> and I made the widow's heart sing for joy.
> I put on righteousness as a garment and it clothed me;
> justice, like a cloak or a turban, wrapped me round.
> I was eyes to the blind
> and feet to the lame;
> I was a father to the needy
> and I took up the stranger's cause.[21]

In the Sinai Covenant, Yahweh chooses Israel as his people
because he loves them, but demands of Israel the highest standard
of justice. This explosive mixture of justice and love dominates
Israel's history. When Israel settles in Canaan, the prophets shock
her leaders by declaring that Yahweh loves justice more than he
loves Israel. When the rich oppress the poor, when merchants
give short change or follow market economics by putting up prices
in time of scarcity, when judges take bribes from the rich and
refuse to hear the poor man's case, and when the kings make unjust
laws and publish burdensome decrees, they condemn such in-
justices as a breach of the Covenant.[22]

When there is grave injustice, the God of the Covenant is not
neutral, but takes the side of the poor and oppressed. The Psalmists
praise Yahweh as the defender of the exploited and defenceless[23]
and when Isaiah puts the nation's leaders on trial before God,
Yahweh appears, not as the impartial judge, but as prosecuting
counsel:

> The Lord comes forward *to argue his case*
> and stands to judge his people.
> The Lord *opens the indictment*
> *against the leaders of his people and their officers:*
> You have ravaged the vineyard (i.e. the nation),
> and the spoils of the poor are in your houses.[24]

The extent of injustice and apostasy[25] convince the prophets
that Israel has turned its back on God. They therefore read current
events as an expression of Yahweh's verdict and sentence. The
imperial expansion of world powers, and the growing threats of
invasion and exile, are the 'day of Yahweh', his sentence of death

on Israel as a sovereign nation. Yahweh's day is a day of judgment, for he has measured the nation with his plumb-line of justice and declared it ripe for demolition.[26]

The judgment is complete. The twin kingdoms of Israel and Judah, divided since the death of Solomon, are in turn invaded and overcome. The former is completely destroyed by Assyria, while the latter, more than a century later, is laid waste and most of her people deported to Babylon.

Yet the exodus experience is not forgotten. In the death throes of Judah, it gives birth to a faith that exile and destruction will not be the end, because Yahweh still loves his people. When Jerusalem is finally surrounded, and battering rams are at the gate, Jeremiah buys a field off one of his kinsfolk, as a sign that one day the land will be re-inhabited. From the despair of exile, Ezekiel sees the breath of God putting new life into the dry bones of his people. An un-named prophet hails Cyrus the Persian's imminent conquest of Babylon as the promise of a new exodus, in which Yahweh will lead his people back from exile to their own land.[27] This new liberation is also an act of supreme forgiveness, of love that goes beyond justice. Yahweh has taken pity on his people, and promises a new Covenant of peace that will never fail.[28]

To sum up, the Old Testament presents Israel's faith in the God who frees slaves, sides with the poor and oppressed, yet loves and forgives his unrighteous people. It believes in a love which goes beyond justice, yet is essential if justice is to be established on earth.

### *Loving justice*

The third strand of Christian thought is not a separate conception of justice but the way in which faith in Jesus Christ views the other two.

The essence of loving justice can be drawn from the story of Zacchaeus and the conversion of St Paul. On his final journey to Jerusalem, Jesus passes through Jericho. There he sees the local superintendent of taxes perched in the fork of a sycamore tree to get a better view of this new prophet from Galilee. Zacchaeus is hated and detested by his fellow-Jews, on three counts. He is collecting taxes for the occupying power of Rome, against which guerrilla patriots are struggling in the desert hills, and so has all the odium of the quisling and collaborator. Because he is soiling his hands by his daily contact with Gentiles, he is also impure and unclean. Finally, because he takes his cut from the taxes he collects, he is widely regarded as an extortioner.

Justice would ignore such a man. The judgment of God would punish him and give him his just deserts. The mercy of God might pardon him – *if he first showed convincing signs of repentance, and changed his way of life.* Jesus goes beyond both mercy and justice by stopping in a crowded street and publicly demonstrating his friendship and respect: 'Zacchaeus, be quick and come down; I must come and stay with you today.'[29] His request for hospitality is not – and would not have seemed – an imposition or a burden. It is a willingness to enter this despicable man's house, touch his unclean hands and utensils, and break bread with him, with all the Eastern connotations of hospitality and fellowship. It is a love, and a faith in persons, that risks failure and rejection in order to try and *create* justice – perhaps because Jesus sensed the longing mixed with shame that prompted Zacchaeus to climb his tree.

In this instance love does create justice, since Zacchaeus gains the courage to give half his possessions to charity and offer four-fold restitution to anyone he has defrauded. But for anyone seriously concerned with God's justice and righteousness, it would seem an unacceptable risk.

It would also border on blasphemy. By the time of Jesus, the passion for Yahweh's righteousness had gathered the weight of sacred tradition in the Torah, the Law of Moses, which regulated the people's daily life in every detail. Though the love of God could be expressed in his mercy, this was the exception proving the rule. In general, the demands of justice stood firm and un-alterable. Like any other conception of justice, God's justice could only be established by upholding and enforcing it – thus demon-strating the goodness of God and the rightness of his righteousness. Justice demanded that wrong be denounced and the guilty punished. To go against this, to do so repeatedly and in public – as Jesus did – *and to claim divine authority for so doing*, was a challenge that no one could ignore. To treat the unjust and un-righteous in the way that Jesus treated Zacchaeus, and to make such treatment a general rule, was an offence against justice. It mocked the faith in God's righteousness for which the Jewish martyrs had suffered and died. Anyone who persisted in such actions, and invoked the name of God, invited the strongest official reaction. He could not be allowed to live. If – by some incredible change in God's purpose – such a person really was the promised Messiah, it was inconceivable that the God of justice and truth would allow his chosen one to be shamed, cursed, and executed for breaking his own law. He would surely intervene in such an unlikely situation, to bring the Messiah down from the cross, so that the people could believe.

This persistence in creative love going before any sign of repentance, combined with a general attitude of freedom towards the Mosaic law, was one of the reasons why Jesus was crucified – by national leaders motivated not merely by political considerations, but by a zeal for God's righteousness and truth.

Saul the Pharisee shared his fellow-countrymen's view of Jesus. In his single-minded zeal for the righteousness of God expressed in the law, it was natural for him to try and stamp out the new sect which had sprung up in devotion to the executed blasphemer. The story of Saul's conversion on the road to Damascus is well known. The key to its significance, and the explanation of such a dramatic change, was his firm belief that in that visionary experience he met the crucified Jesus now risen and alive. Within the logic of Paul's faith and thought-world, this could only have one explanation. It meant that the universal awakening of the dead, long expected at the end of the present age, had now begun.[30] It meant that God himself had raised Jesus from death into a new and transformed life, thereby saying 'yes' to all that Jesus had said and done in his name. Among other things, this meant that the God whose righteousness Saul prized so highly had said 'yes' to Jesus' treatment of people like Zacchaeus.

When Paul thought through the meaning of his conversion-experience, he therefore concluded that in Jesus of Nazareth, God had demonstrated his justice in a revolutionary way, by loving and accepting all alike, just and unjust, without conditions, in order to overcome alienation and injustice and reconcile people to God and to each other. This new conception of a love that risks all, and accepts death and rejection, to try and create justice and bring

every Zacchaeus down from his tree, solved a problem for which
the law had no answer. For the more zealously it pointed to God's
righteousness, the more conclusively did it show the believer how
far he fell short of that righteousness in his own life. Paul could
therefore speak of God's new demonstration of his justice as an
act of liberation.[31]

Thus, the Christian experience of God, in the cross and resurrection of Christ, is of a love that surpasses justice in the hope that
justice can at last be created. This love accepts people as they
are, reaching out to every human being on earth, offering forgiveness, fellowship and hope, endlessly and without distinction, as
Christ seeks to draw all humanity to himself.[32]

## *Justice in Christian faith*

The three strands of Christian thought are a unity, each of which
contributes something to the others.

Natural justice has much in common with the rational theory
of justice as fairness. Both start from the fundamental equality
and individual worth of every human person and work towards
quite similar principles of justice. The difference is that for the
rationalist the basic conviction is a matter of moral intuition, while
for the Christian it stems from a basic article of faith.

The Old Testament tradition of Yahweh's saving justice shows
that God's salvation is not only personal, but also political,
economic and historical. It leads us to expect that the Lord of
history is still working to establish justice, and that he is neither
absent from the events of our own time nor neutral towards them.
Since it became obvious that God is not directly involved in
changing the local weather or helping British armies to defeat the
Kaiser, Christians have been chary about pointing too glibly to
his unseen finger in daily events. But laying aside crankiness and
superficiality, the attempt must still be made. From all the expertise
of economics, ecology, sociology and political science, Christian
faith should try to understand the significant changes which are
taking place around us. It should then interpret them from its
knowledge of God's justice and love.[33] There is no reason to suppose, for example, that the present prosperity of the rich north
of the globe, or the culture and institutions of Western democracies,

are of permanent or absolute value in the sight of God. If our way of life turns out to be founded on global suffering and injustice, we should not be surprised if those foundations are shaken. We should prepare to meet our God[34] and expect to see, in the most traumatic events, signs of both justice and love, judgment and hope.

The Old Testament also reveals a God who has a *passion* for justice, while Jesus blesses those who hunger and thirst to see right prevail.[35] For the Christian, a passion for justice cannot therefore be dismissed as 'the politics of envy' if it is seeking to establish what is right, fair and good.

Finally, the God of saving justice is neither neutral nor unbiased. He meets us personally in our suffering and exploited neighbour.[36] His justice means, 'not the balance of civil claims or the enforcement of contracts but *outrageous partisanship* for the poor and helpless, a concern to lift them up, to empower them as equal members of the community, to give them their humanity in the covenant.'[37] To be partisan is to take sides, not peer round every aspect of a question in order to reach a 'balanced view'. There are times when one-sidedness is the only way to work credibly with people who are unjustly treated or oppressed.

On the other hand, the New Testament reveals a love which goes beyond justice and loves the unrighteous, the unjust and the enemy. Christian action for justice therefore lives in a tension between one-sided commitment and objective truth, between an outrageous partisanship which takes sides and love for whoever one sides against.

The New Testament experience also confirms the insights of natural justice. It guarantees the unique yet equal value of every person as loved and accepted to the uttermost through the death and resurrection of Christ. In today's world, such acceptance and respect cannot be limited to personal relationships. In everything we do – buying and selling, working or going on strike, eating more or eating less, spending, saving or giving away, breathing or polluting the air – we are invisibly related to distant neighbours. Our neighbours are not only individual persons, but classes, races and nations. In such a world Christian love has to be expressed, not only in service and caring towards individuals, but in systems and structures which champion the weak and defenceless and are as fair as possible to all. In an interlocking world, *love of neighbour has to take shape as justice*.

### Problems of rational justice

The value of such thinking to non-Christians must be judged by the reader. There are, however, two questions which a Christian understanding of justice must put to any rational one.

Firstly, why should the rational person care about posterity? Rawls assumes that the persons making their agreement on principles of justice are heads of families who must consider the next generation. This is a reasonable assumption, since most people do care about their children's welfare, and many also care about the prospects for their grandchildren. But a rational theory cannot easily explain why anyone should worry about the distant future, even when it recognizes that such concern is now an urgent necessity if humanity is to survive. Christian faith has a coherent hope for the future, and also sees humanity as having the care and management of this planet in perpetuity under God.

Secondly, can a rational theory give the rationalist a strong enough motive to struggle for justice in an unjust world, or account for acts of love that witness to justice by going far beyond it? On Rawls' theory, individuals have a natural duty 'to assist in the establishment of just arrangements ... at least when this can be done with little cost to ourselves.'[38] In the real world, it is doubtful whether that degree of commitment will do much to achieve justice. Yet anything beyond it is classed as a 'supererogatory act', and such acts are only mentioned in the theory for the sake of completeness. To have a passion for justice or sacrifice oneself for justice's sake is not rational. Yet it is sometimes necessary if justice is to be attained. If 'justice which is only justice soon degenerates into less than justice', and 'must be saved by something more than justice'[39], then the rationalist needs something more than rational theory.

This 'something more' is not necessarily a Christian faith, though Christian faith can provide it. Other trans-rational understandings of justice raise such questions. On 11 June 1963 the Venerable Thich Quang-Duc, a Buddhist monk, doused himself with petrol and burned himself to death in a Saigon street. Such an action, in Buddhist terms, is not suicide, nor even protest. It aims to move the hearts of the oppressor by witnessing to the monk's determination to protect his people. 'What he really aims at is the expression of his will and determination, not death.... The monk who burns himself has lost neither courage nor hope; nor does he desire non-existence,' – for life is not confined to a human span of sixty or eighty or a hundred years. On the contrary, such a monk is courageous and hopeful and aspires to something good in the future. 'He believes in the good fruition of his act of self-sacrifice for the sake of others.'[40]

Almost exactly twenty years earlier, Franz Jägerstätter was beheaded in a Berlin prison. He was an Austrian peasant-farmer from the remote village of St Radegund, a lay Catholic, happily married, with three daughters, the eldest not quite six. Alone, and against the advice and persuasion of his church, his family, and the civil and military authorities, he came to the conviction that he could not fight in Hitler's unjust war. In the final letter to his family, written a few hours before his execution, he says, in part:

> All my dear ones, the hour comes ever closer when I will be giving my soul back to God, the Master.... I would have liked ... to spare you the pain and sorrow that you must bear because of me. But you know we must love God even more than family, and we must lose everything dear and worthwhile here on earth rather than commit even the slightest offence against God...
>
> Many actually believe quite simply that things have to be the way they are. If this should happen to mean that they are obliged to commit injustice, then they believe that others are responsible.... But if I know in advance that I cannot accept and obey everything I would promise under that oath, then I would be guilty of a lie. For this reason I am convinced that it is still best that I speak the truth, even if it costs me my life.[41]

Both Christian and Buddhist went far beyond justice for the sake of justice, believing that justice and truth could be served in no other way. A rational theory is not complete until it takes this kind of conviction into account.

## *Summary and conclusion*

The meaning of social justice can be summarized as follows:

Justice calls for the establishment of a society – on both a global and national scale – where each person has an equal right to the most extensive basic liberties compatible with a like liberty for all, where social and economic inequalities are so arranged that they are to the greatest benefit of the least advantaged, and where they are linked with positions and appointments which are open to all through fair equality of opportunity.

In such a society, justice puts limits on the kind of orders a person may give or receive. It ensures that people who have authority and power are directly answerable to those beneath them, or whom their decisions affect.

A just society does not level down natural differences of talent and ability. It accepts such natural inequalities, but treats them as a common asset rather than an individual possession. Private ownership of anything is a secondary privilege, not a fundamental right. Private ownership of goods, land, wealth, or the means of production and distribution, *has to be justified* (if it is allowed at all) as being of greatest benefit to the least advantaged.

A just society calls for a sharing of superfluous wealth, and reckons what is superfluous by the needs of the poor. It is marked by a continuing redistribution of wealth and power towards its poorest and least favoured members, and by a positive discrimination which tries as far as possible to make up for their natural, social, cultural, political and economic disadvantages.

A just society is based on the fundamental equality of worth of every human being. It shows in its structures and institutions a respect for the dignity and worth of every one of its members.

The establishment and maintenance of a just society calls for a passion for justice based not on envy, but on the determination to see right prevail. It needs, from some of its members at least, acts of love that love the unjust and go beyond justice, as a witness to justice and truth.

The dialogue approach to education springs from the same roots as this understanding of social justice. It too regards each human being as a knowing subject, precious, unique, and fundamentally equal with others. It believes that each person has the right to find his or her voice, develop critical consciousness and become more fully human by knowing and changing the world.

In a world of grave injustice, where all yet have a fundamental equality, education for justice will therefore seek to increase people's knowledge of injustice and inequality, to widen their range of comparison, and to create a critical consciousness which turns grievance or guilt into hopeful and constructive action. Such education is not a neutral process that simply 'gives people the facts'. Yet because it is concerned with justice, it must itself be just.[42] It cannot be a propaganda exercise that gives facts-with-slogans and tells or persuades people what to do. It has to be a dialogue holding together conviction and commitment with openness and trust.

# 5

# Justice, Power and Conflict

The relations between groups (are) predominantly political rather than ethical, that is, they will be determined by the proportion of power which each group possesses at least as much as by any rational or moral appraisal of the comparative needs and claims of each group. ... when collective power ... exploits weakness, it can never be dislodged unless power is raised against it.... Conflict is inevitable, and in this conflict power must be challenged by power.

Reinhold Niebuhr[1]

One obstacle to social justice is the difficulty of standing in another person's shoes. Suppose that a husband-and-wife team of Canadian hydrologists is visiting a remote village in Africa. Their task is to find the best and most economical way of bringing good drinking water to the village, and obtaining the villagers' approval for the scheme. The cheapest way will probably be to divert water from the nearby stream into a reservoir and purify it with chemicals. Well-boring is impossible, and to take a pipeline from the spring higher up the mountain would cost twice as much to install and maintain. Before visiting the village, they learn that the stream water is dangerously polluted, and that they should avoid sitting on the ground because it is infested with mangoe worms.

The villagers await their arrival. They want good drinking water, but know from long experience that the nearby stream is the home of evil spirits. Several people have died from drinking its water and their wisest men have been unable to drive the spirits away. They therefore prefer to get water from the spring two miles up the mountain. It is their custom to greet visitors with only a *limp* handshake, to offer them a cup of water as a sign of friendship, to sit cross-legged in a circle on the ground to signify their equality, and – except among close relatives – for men to speak only to men and women only to women.

What will happen when the visitors arrive? Even if they avoid giving offence by refusing the proffered water, giving hearty North American handshakes all round, talking indiscriminately to everyone and refusing to sit on the ground, it will take much time and patience for visitors and villagers to respect each other and enter each other's world.[2] Magnified and multiplied many times, such barriers of culture and language make it difficult for people in different groups or communities to understand each other, or to weigh the justice of other claims. 'No man will ever be so intelligent as to see the needs of others as vividly as he recognises his own.'[3]

### Vested interests

Another fundamental obstacle to the establishment of justice is the clash of vested interests. In the daily newspapers a report calling for smaller classes and better-paid teachers will probably have been prepared by a teachers' union. Letters defending the policy of military regimes tend to come from the embassy concerned. Evidence against aerosol sprays is gathered by environmental lobbyists. Evidence that atomic power stations are leakproof is supplied by the Atomic Energy Authority. No one has the right to be cynical about such limitations, because we all share them. The difference is that our own particular claim usually seems to us unbiased, irrefutable, and indistinguishable from the common good.

The most serious clashes of interest are political and economic, and the most persistent are clashes of interest between different social classes. In such conflicts of interest, the individual person almost inevitably takes his attitudes from the group to which he belongs. By choice and situation, we spend most time with, and take most notice of, 'people like us' – people with similar standards, life-style and experience. Since our standard of living is affected by the outcome of economic clashes of interest, we find it as easy to see the justice of our own position as it is hard to see anything but cussedness, greed, envy and unreasonableness in the claims of the opposing group. Where white collar workers see inefficiency, overmanning and resistance to new ideas, the man on the assembly line sees the threat of redundancy and unemployment.

A serious clash of interests is not like a Quaker Meeting. The groups involved may not have a common vision of society, nor even a basic agreement about what the problem is. Though the opposing sides may meet and talk to each other, they cannot reach agreement solely by reasoned argument and discussion. Their conflict of interests is precisely that – a *battle*, in which words, protests, votes, lock-outs, boycotts and strikes take the place of quarterstaffs, guns and swords. Statistics, evidence, reasoned arguments or moral and religious convictions will all be used to gain support or discomfit the opponent. Conflicts of interest are resolved by victory, defeat, agreed compromise, the discovery of agreement at a deeper level or the imposition of peace by a third party. Because it is backed by armed strength, the most obvious third party is the government, which lays the ground rules of such conflicts and can often impose a particular solution. Thus, *though moral persuasion and reasoned argument can play an important role in clashes of interest, they are not sufficient to resolve them.*

### The will to power

A third obstacle to the achievement of justice is that those who wield power, including governments, cannot always use that power justly. In both individuals and groups, there is a *will to power*. Sometimes it is a naked desire to dominate, to be a Hitler, a Stalin, or a dictatorial bureaucrat or boss. Sometimes it is a vested interest that asserts itself beyond reasonable limits. Often, tragically, it is a sense of responsibility or zeal for justice which becomes blinkered by the limits of sympathy, stampeded by shortness of time, and poisoned by flattery or fear of displacement.

'*All* power corrupts' – and power corrupts at all levels. There is a close connection between self-denial and self-aggrandizement. The father who makes sacrifices for his children is practising self-denial. Because he loves them, he wants them to grow, develop, and be the best they can possibly be. The more they do so, the more he is pleased – but his simple pleasure is coloured by the fact that their ability, success, or kindness also reflect favourably on him and flatter his ego.

Patriotism is similarly double-faced. The patriot unselfishly gives his loyalty to a wider cause, and puts his country's interest above his own. But in doing so, he also feels a sense of importance, a reflected glory from his country's power and influence. Governments which face internal unrest almost invariably try to defuse opposition by some act of national self-assertion – a war, a border dispute, a trade agreement, or even a peace mission to settle someone else's conflicts. Such actions appeal to both the unselfishness and the self-glorification of their people, asking them to sink their differences 'for the good of our nation'. Similarly, the individual works unselfishly for his team, his party, and his organization, yet longs to see it have prestige and power in its relations with others, to succeed, dominate or rule. Justice can therefore only be achieved if the will to power is regulated and controlled. It is a bargain struck between reason and power.

### The meaning of power

Power is, very loosely, the ability to control or change either people or things. Positively, power implies choice – the ability to choose what to buy, eat or wear, how to spend your time, where to live and what work to do for a living. Power implies responsibility – the freedom and capacity to plan your life and make your own decisions. Finally, power implies the capacity to give. A person's self-respect is increased when she can give to others, whether by providing for her children or buying a gift for a friend. The powerless are those who have no freedom of choice, no responsibility or share in decisions, and little that they can give to others. Injustice arises when responsibility, participation and freedom of choice are held by the few at the expense of the many.

Power over others is of three interrelated kinds.[4] The first, and most fundamental, is physical or political power. It is expressed in one person's muscular strength over another, and in the coercion that is the necessary foundation of society. It is symbolized and enforced by law courts, police, prisons, and the armed forces. In a democracy, coercion is often beneath the surface. This breeds the illusion that democratic government is achieved purely by persuasion, and that people accept majority decisions because they think the majority is right. In reality, the majority has its way, not because minorities respect its superior virtue, but because – and as long as – its votes are the expression of strength. If the majority loses its hold on the institutions of power, or if a minority is desperate or courageous enough, the mere number of votes will not prevent a conflict. In times of crisis, physical power quickly comes to the surface in the most settled democracy. Civil rights are suspended, news is censored, internment without trial replaces imprisonment, and army patrols appear on the streets.

Economic power is expressed in such phrases as, 'We are withdrawing our labour from tomorrow night' or 'The management regrets that your services will not be required after Friday'. It is the power to control or influence the production of society's wealth, and affect people's ability to earn their living. It is the power of the purse, power over daily bread. It is closely related to political power, and usually goes hand in hand with it. If economic power in a society shifts from one class to another (e.g. from artistocratic landowners to merchants in the towns) political power usually follows it, though not without a struggle.

Cultural power is just as real, but less easy to measure. It is power over people's minds. It is the ability to persuade people to accept your view of the world, your estimate of what they need and ought to want, your expert advice about their problems. A friend of mine taught as a volunteer in a West African school. At first, she was worried to find that the pupils were always late for lessons. She stressed the importance of being on time, and tried to encourage punctuality by installing a clock in the classroom. Gradually, she began to enter the cultural world of the people, where sun and seasons are the only timekeepers, and where it is more important to stop and greet a neighbour on the road than to arrive at school by a particular number on the white lady's clock. Quite unconsciously, and with good intentions, she had attempted to exercise cultural power – by trying to persuade the people to accept her understanding of the importance of time. An African teacher who came to Britain and succeeded in banishing clocks and timetables from the classroom would be exercising cultural power in reverse – though historically the dominating flow of energy has been the other way.

From an educational point of view, cultural power is particularly important. The development of critical consciousness helps to free people from all kinds of cultural domination, whether deliberate or unconscious. Where cultural power is the instrument of economic and political injustice, to develop a critical consciousness is a first step towards freedom, and one of the main tasks of education for justice.

## *Justice as equal power*

The limits to our understanding of another person's situation, the clash of vested interests, and the will to power of individuals and groups, make it impossible to establish justice by reason and persuasion alone. If the relations between groups are determined as much by the proportion of power which each group possesses as by rational and moral ideals,[5] it follows that justice between different organizations, vested interests, power groups and nations, can only be guaranteed if they meet each other with equal strength. *Equal worth can only be established by equal power.* 'My dear Christian brothers', said a Peruvian political scientist to an English house church, 'You can never govern the world with good wishes and good counsels. It is a question of justice, of legislation, of a balance of power. If we Latin-Americans don't unite and create a United States of South America, we will never get better treatment from North America. Therefore be careful my dear friends. The only thing you can do for us is to help us to become stronger and stronger, until we are as strong, as heavy, as you.'

Equality of power is primarily political and economic. But cultural power matters too. Not long ago, the Education Committee of a large English city agreed that parents in a working-class area should participate fully in the running of a new nursery centre. All parents of under-fives were invited to a public meeting, at which they elected representatives on to the management committee. Parent representatives made up half the committee and had full voting rights. In terms of their voting strength, they had an equal say in appointing staff for the centre, fixing its opening hours, and deciding on its overall policy. In practice, the parents were less articulate, and less familiar with committee procedures, than the councillors and officials. The latter had unquestioned expert knowledge and also prepared the agenda. Despite goodwill, and the serious intent of everyone involved, the balance of power shifted very little. 'The formal structure obscures the extent to which politicians and professionals retain control over important decisions.'[6]

## Clinging to power

Vested interests, the limits to our understanding of others' needs, and the will to power, all combine to make people afraid of losing their power over others. 'It is highly unlikely', says a South African social scientist in a careful study of his country, 'that whites will share power and privilege with blacks without a good deal of pressure being brought to bear upon them or without it being in their self-interest to do so.'[7] The point is made in more general terms by black American Frederick Douglass in his West India Emancipation Speech of 1857 –

> Those who profess to favor freedom yet deprecate agitation, are men who want crops without plowing up the ground; they want rain without thunder and lightning. They want the ocean without the awful roar of its many waters ... *Power concedes nothing without demand.* It never did and it never will. Find out just what any people will quietly submit to and you have found out the exact measure of injustice and wrong which will be imposed upon them, and these will continue till they are resisted with either words, or blow, or with both. *The limits of tyrants are prescribed by the endurance of those whom they oppress.*[8]

The main reason why power concedes nothing without demand is not that some individuals are power-hungry, nor that there is a conscious, organized conspiracy by gnomes of Zurich or reds under the bed. It is that the race, class and organizations we belong to help to shape our attitudes and behaviour. Our limited ability to understand another's needs makes us more inclined to hold on to what we have. If the 'others' are people we rarely see and never meet because they belong to a different social group, their needs will always seem less *real*, less pressing than our own. 'Even without conscious collusion or naked self-interest', says a study of the US anti-poverty programme, 'the values, tastes and distastes of middle-class America naturally conspire to render as little to the less fortunate as its own security and conscience will allow.'[9]

Another reason why power concedes nothing without demand lies in the difference between personal and structural relationships. As already indicated we grow up into a complex world of human culture. One of the things we learn as we grow is that certain types of relationship between people are normal, 'obvious' and taken-for-granted. We assume that marriage means a monogamous relationship rather than, say, polyandry. We grow into particular economic relationships – between shareholders, management and workers for example – which we accept as part of the social landscape, as natural as grass and as immovable as the mountains. Within such structural relationships there is, of course, an element of personal freedom. If we want our employees to do something we can either ask them politely, or shout at them. We can pay them higher or lower wages than the norm, and provide better or worse working conditions than average. Because we are aware of such possibilities we tend to apply moral questions to the freedom we have rather than the structure in which that freedom operates. We take the structural relationships of our society for granted, and argue about whether we are being fair or considerate within them. It is very difficult for us even to consider the possibility that the structure itself might be unjust, and even more difficult to do anything towards changing it if it is.[10]

With this insight, it is perhaps easier to understand why earlier centuries witnessed long debates about how to behave justly towards one's slaves (without questioning the institution of slavery), or why the commanders of twentieth-century concentration camps can be loving and considerate to their family and friends (without ever questioning the morality of torture, forced labour or the 'final solution'). During the Vietnam war a news magazine carried a cartoon strip with the following series of captions: 'I only work on the assembly line' – 'I only drive a delivery truck from the factory' – 'I only take delivery of the goods' – 'I only help to load the plane' – 'I only give clearance for take-off' – 'I only pilot an aircraft' – 'I only press a button'. The last picture showed Vietnamese villagers saying . . . '. . . And we get killed by the bomb'.

Held in the invisible web of such structural relationships, it is difficult for the beneficiaries of social injustice to understand their relationship with its victims. In such a position, we find it hard to realize, much less accept that our privilege might be held at the cost of other people's suffering, or that the structural relationships could be different or more just. The demand for justice is hardly heard, and, if heard, resisted and resented. After cataloguing the statistics of inequality between white and black in America, Stokely Carmichael and Charles Hamilton conclude that the black community is dominated by the institutional racism and vested interests of the white power structure. 'This is not to say that every single white American consciously oppresses black people. *He does not need to*' – the web of economic and political relationships does it for him.[11]

Privileged groups in a society also cling to their power because, over a period of time, they come to take their privileges for granted and regard them as a right. Their advantages come to be thought of as normal and proper, sanctioned by time, custom and history. Proposals to change the situation arouse moral indignation – 'Who do they think they are? I've worked hard for my standard of living!' Elaborate doctrines are developed to defend and justify the *status quo*. Rarely does anyone say, except as a last resort, 'I've got this and I'm hanging on to it'. People with privileges almost always need to convince themselves that they deserve them. Thus, paradoxically, justice is accepted as an ideal in the act of justifying injustice. Power and privilege try to hide their nakedness with a cloak of morality – partly because moral standards are still regarded as important, and partly because economic and political power buttress themselves with cultural power, by trying to convince the poor and deprived that unequal rewards and privileges *ought* to be where they are.

## No escape from conflict

If justice can only be guaranteed by equality of power, and if power is never shared or surrendered by moral persuasion alone, *it follows that justice in society can only be established through conflict*. 'There is as yet no evidence that a privileged class, which yields advantage after advantage peacefully, will finally yield the very basis of its special position in society without conflict.'[12] Reason, morality, and persuasion can ease the conflict, but they cannot wish it away.

It is important to note that conflict means any form of struggle or clash of interests and does not necessarily involve physical violence. In the inner city areas of the United States, for example, the only weapons available to the poorest people are their weight of numbers and the disconcerting effect of publicity on the city fathers if they make a fuss. Such modest firepower has to be used to the full to bring change. Experience shows that negotiation will only bear fruit if backed by the possibility of bringing such resources to bear.[13]

Where there is grave injustice, conflict suppressed means future conflict intensified. In the study of South Africa previously quoted, the social scientists saw two possible pathways to change. One would be to relax the barrier of apartheid and allow selected individual blacks to move up the social scale. This might be relatively peaceful, but would not bring any real change by the standards of social justice. The other kind of change necessarily involves a conflict between the privileged and underprivileged classes leading to the improved position of black South Africans as a whole. 'The question is not whether there will be conflict or no conflict, but rather what the intensity of the friction or conflict will be.' The white reaction will determine whether the conflict is open, unregulated, and violent, or whether it can be channelled into institutions and bargaining arrangements through which black South Africans can gain specific changes to improve their position.[14]

### Taking sides

If justice can only be established through conflict, then no one who is bound up in the webs of structural injustice can claim to be neutral. The crucial question is not, 'Should I get involved?' but, 'Whose side are you on?' If a multinational company wants to build an oil terminal on the Scottish coast the local church has three options. It can give warm support, claim to be neutral, or come out in opposition. Whatever the rights and wrongs may be, the first two courses have the same effect – they support the company's efforts, whether by encouragement or default. 'Neutrality is a way of giving in to power and money pressures, of making straight the way of the powerful.'[15]

Conflict cannot be avoided, and neutrality is impossible. In an attempt to establish justice, taking sides is often the price of effective action. One of the main lessons of American community development programmes during the 1960s was that no reform movement could bypass conflicts of interest or survey them from some 'objective' height. To be effective, a reforming organization had to take sides and surrender any claim to universal authority.[16]

This general experience was confirmed by the Home Office Community Development Project in Coventry (1970–1975). For the first year or so of its life some members of the team acted as advocates of local causes, while others tried to represent and explain the corporation's policies to the residents. Despite the clear separation of roles, both residents and council officials were uneasy about the position of the team. *'Both the local authority and the residents were concerned to know "whose side" we were on ... we had to choose* between acting as agents of established power or of community power.'[17] In the event, they chose to identify themselves with the feelings and interests of the local residents, as the only way of being accepted by them and working with them for change.

### Summary and conclusions

The argument of this chapter has been that because of the limits on our ability to see another's situation, the clash of vested interests, and the will to power of individuals and groups, social justice is a bargain struck between power and reason. Equality of worth can only be guaranteed by equality of power. Since power is never conceded without demand, social justice has to be established through conflict. Reason and morality can ease the conflict, but cannot wish it away. In such conflicts, no one can claim to be neutral. The worker for justice will often have to be partisan, and take sides.

This argument leads to two main conclusions.[18] Firstly, there is a fundamental clash of interests between the victims of a grave injustice and those who benefit from it. It is not lessened by the fact that the most privileged individuals often feel trapped by the structural relationships which bind them. Ask the lowest-paid factory worker where the power lies in his company and he will probably answer, 'With the management'. Ask anyone on the board of directors and they will probably reply that real power lies with the trade unions, the government, the shareholders or the customer. In a modern society, power is diffused and no one's power is absolute. Confronted with the facts of poverty and injustice at home and abroad, members of the most privileged and comfortable groups spread their hands in bewilderment and cry, 'what can we do?'. Education for justice must take seriously both the suffering of the victims and the bewilderment of the beneficiaries, but it cannot ignore the great divide between them.

Secondly, the relation between the ideal of social justice and the realities of power and conflict is dialectical – a unity of opposites, where each needs the other. Without a clear understanding of power and conflict, the person who seeks justice becomes naive, ineffective and sentimental. Without a vision of justice for all, the passionate activist becomes despairing or cynical, and the struggle itself becomes an endless treadmill of revolution where the victims of injustice overthrow injustice in order to inflict it on others.

The clear-sighted worker for justice will therefore take sides in this or that social conflict. She will try to win a more equal sharing of power, not as an end in itself, but in order to increase the influence of reason and morality. *She will seek equality of power in order to establish mutual respect and equality of worth.* She will struggle for justice as wholeheartedly and effectively as possible. But her choice of 'weapons' (whether reasoned argument, campaigns, protests, civil disobedience or even armed force) will never be determined solely by the need to win, but also by the need to overcome hostility and resentment after victory, to minimize revenge and resentment, and to create new relationships based on justice for all. She will make the daily compromises between justice and power, yet hope and work for a new order where there are neither masters nor slaves, beneficiaries nor victims, oppressors nor oppressed.

# 6

# The Marks of Cultural Oppression

People wish to be settled: only as they are unsettled is there any hope
for them.                                    Ralph Waldo Emerson

The previous chapter argued that there is a fundamental opposition
between the beneficiaries of injustice and its victims. The first
problem in describing this opposition is to know what sorts of
situation we are talking about. Rather than generalize into abstrac-
tion, I shall think mainly in terms of the extreme and clear-cut
situations in Latin America and South Africa, and the damaging
bleakness of poverty and powerlessness in the big cities of Britain
and the USA. The symptoms described below probably apply more
widely, but where, how far, and with what modifications, are
questions best left to the reader.

The second problem is to find an acceptable way of describing
the groups or classes of people on opposite sides of the great divide.
In a situation of structural injustice, one group has power over
another, and uses it (knowingly or unknowingly) to dominate and
control. One should therefore say that one group dominates or
oppresses the other, rather than talk vaguely about the 'privileged'
or 'advantaged' and the 'underprivileged', 'disadvantaged' or
'deprived'. To speak of oppression, oppressors and oppressed
commonly meets two objections. One is that words like oppression
are too extreme a label for poverty and powerlessness in our own
cities. In fact, the dictionary definitions are quite wide. To oppress
is not merely to 'govern tyranically' and 'overwhelm with irresist-
ible power' but also to 'lie heavy on' and generally 'weigh down
(spirits, imagination, etc.)'. Remembering the observation that
many individual white Americans do not consciously oppress

blacks because the social structure does it for them,[1] it does not seem too exaggerated to think that our *social structure* could 'keep people under by coercion' or 'subject them to continual cruelty or injustice'. To underline the point that oppression is not necessarily or always a conscious action by individuals, I shall speak interchangeably of oppressors and oppressed or of the beneficiaries and victims of injustice. A second objection is that to divide the world into beneficiaries–oppressors and victims–oppressed is too sharp a polarization, and that there are many other, more subtle relationships to be considered, both in and between classes and groups of people. The aim of this chapter is however to highlight a crucially important relationship, not suggest that it is the only one.

### *The image of inferiority*

In his parable of political and economic oppression, Tolstoy pictures himself sitting on another man's back, choking him and weighing him down, yet doing everything possible to make things easier and lighten the load – except by getting off. The Brazilian cartoonist, Claudius Ceccon, has given us an equally sharp portrait of cultural oppression. It shows the silhouetted head of a black man with lowered eyes and furrowed brow and, seated comfortably inside his brain, the smiling, cigar-smoking image of his white boss.

The oppressor housed in the mind of the culturally oppressed person may be a composite image of actual people who tell him that he is inferior, worthless, a scrounger or a layabout. Or it may stand for the impersonal structures of a society which can offer him no job, imprisons him on low pay, requires him to be grateful and deferential towards the welfare authorities and labels him a failure because he is illiterate or has no paper qualifications. Or it may be a mixture of both. In any case, the effect is the same. The victim of injustice takes inside himself the conviction, imposed on him from outside, that he is valueless and ignorant. 'A black man is and always will be inferior to the white', said a Xhosa factory worker to a black theological student. Asked why his people were lacking in motivation for self-help development, a Zulu community worker replied, 'Sad to say, I blame the whites for this.

Our people were told that their minds were so inferior that they could not do anything, *and they have nursed this in their minds.* They have learnt to be beggars rather than workers. They say, this can only be done by the white man, not us.'

The verdict of South African social scientists is equally emphatic, and not limited to their own society:

As in many authoritarian societies, or in societies characterized by vast social and economic inequality, patterns of interaction are self-reinforcing. The wealth, education and confidence of the average white tend to give him an advantage in any interaction with blacks, which in turn makes the blacks feel inferior, producing among the latter low morale, a lack of self-confidence, dispiritedness and apathy.

The report concludes that these psychological characteristics of the oppressed group are 'functional for the maintenance of the system.'[2]

In Latin America, too, Paulo Freire has documented the 'culture of silence' imposed on descendants of the original inhabitants by centuries of repression.[3] 'The peasant feels inferior to the boss,' one such person told him, 'because the boss seems to be the only one who knows things and is able to run things'. 'The peasant begins to get courage to overcome his dependence,' said another, 'when he realizes that he is dependent. Until then, he goes along with the boss and says, "What can I do? I'm only a peasant."'[4] In the cultural circle, such people are at first shy and afraid to speak. Since they have always been allowed only to listen and obey, they distrust both themselves and the educator who attempts a problem-posing dialogue. 'Excuse us, sir,' they say after a while, 'we who don't know should keep quiet and listen to you who know.'[5]

In less extreme fashion, but from similar roots, the conviction of inferiority saps the will of many people in European and American cities. In the United States, many of the poorest town dwellers, who have nothing to lose but their chains, are too closely chained psychologically to take the risks of action or even believe in the possibility of change.[6] In Britain 'contrary to the hopes of the left and the fears of the right, there is but limited dissent and disorder from the poor.' Many remain passive and inactive, not least because they accept without question the ruling dogma of self-help. Convinced that anyone who *really* tries can find work and better themselves, they come to believe that their unemployment is a reflection, not of the state of the national economy and regional movements of industrial capital, but of their own personal inadequacy. The general belief that everyone who tries can get on in life eats into the poverty-trapped person's view of themselves. People feel a shame and guilt at being poor which – in the vast majority of cases – is quite unrelated to their true economic position.[7]

The victims of cultural oppression are usually also dominated in economic and political ways. The conviction that they are inferior is rarely completely accepted, however, and does battle subconsciously with anger and frustration at the oppressor groups or the oppressive society. Because the oppressed person dares not vent this anger vertically against the oppressors, cannot find a clear target for it, or dares not admit it to consciousness, it is apt to lash out horizontally, in inexplicable squabbles between neighbours, gang warfare, vandalism and faction fighting.[8] Before the peasant discovers his true situation, 'he lets off steam at home, where he shouts at his children, beats them, and despairs. He complains about his wife and thinks everything is dreadful. He doesn't let off steam with the boss because he thinks the boss is a superior being. Lots of times, the peasant gives vent to his sorrows by drinking.'[9]

The imposed conviction of inferiority breeds apathy, and can lead to a pattern of life which reinforces middle class prejudice. In his study of a black ghetto area in America, Jules Henry was struck by the apparently random behaviour of the poorest people. They appeared to have no future goals or aim in life. From a middle class person's viewpoint, such behaviour was both illogical and reprehensible. Most middle class people have a sense of their own worth, and a sense of achievement based on past success. They therefore expect that their lives will change and can plan their activities in a desired direction. Organized activity, directed to some future goal, is a logical pattern of behaviour.

By contrast, the people in the ghetto had little self-esteem, no sense of past achievement on which to build, and therefore no conviction that life could ever change. Their behaviour followed its own logic – the logic of survival, of doing, from moment to moment, in apparently random fashion, *whatever gave them the most intense sensation of being alive.* Henry concludes that, 'Hope separates the free from the slaves, the middle and upper classes from much of the lower class, the hopeful from the hopeless.'[10] This insight may help to explain the fiestas, 'spending sprees', and very often, the generosity and hospitality of the poor.

### The myth of superior virtue

On the other side of the great divide, the beneficiaries of injustice almost always have a psychological need to believe that the victims are inferior. In South Africa and Latin America, this is openly stated, and unspokenly assumed, by whites speaking about Coloureds and Africans[11] and the urban middle class speaking about the peasant. An Afrikaaner Professor of Theology solemnly explained to me that the Coloured Representative Council had to be packed with government nominees because the Coloureds were not educated enough to act responsibly and might be stirred up by agitators. Previous contact with the articulate and capable people he was talking about put this viewpoint in perspective, as also the comment, by a white clergyman, that 'Coloured people find it harder to pass exams than Europeans do. They are very practical people, but we can't expect from them what we can of a European.' As Reinhold Niebuhr observed more than forty years ago:

> ... it has always been the habit of privileged groups to deny the oppressed classes every opportunity for the cultivation of innate capacities and then to accuse them of lacking what they have been denied the right to acquire.[12]

In Southern Africa, earlier convictions of white superiority are being shaken, and white solidarity is maintained more by the twin bogeys of violence and Communism than any *genuine* belief in the frequent appeals to maintain 'Christian civilization'.[13] In the case of more stable societies, it has already been argued that people with economic and political privileges almost always need to convince themselves that they deserve them. 'If the argument is to be plausible ... it must be proved or assumed that the under-privileged classes would not have the same capacity for rendering the same service if given the opportunity.'[14] In the early nineteenth century, the British and American middle class creed of thrift and hard work sprang naturally from its own economic and social position. It was easy for them to believe that the extreme poverty of the workers was caused, not by inequalities of economic power, but simply by their laziness and improvidence – though as the evidence mounted, such beliefs became more like dishonest pretension. They saw their superiority in terms, not merely of skill and foresight, but of moral virtue. 'That you have property', said one, 'is proof of industry and foresight on your part or your father's; that you have nothing is a judgment on your laziness and vices or on your improvidence. The world is a moral world; which it would not be if virtue and vice received the same rewards.'[15]

## *A cycle of deprivation?*

In modern times, the belief that poverty is caused by the inferiority of the poor has reappeared in a more detached and subtle guise. In 1963 the North Carolina Fund coined the idea of a 'cycle of deprivation' to explain the persistence of poverty amid affluence. Children of poor and inadequate parents, it suggests, start with a disadvantage and rapidly fall behind. They drop out of school and grow up unable to give their own children either a stable home or a good start in life.

In many individual cases this is undoubtedly true. As I write, a television documentary has recently charted the legacy of love-lessness from the grown-up child of a 1952 broken marriage to her own daughter, taken into care in 1975. But as an explanation of continued poverty in whole areas of city and countryside, the poverty-cycle theory is less convincing. In 1969 the Home Office began the national Community Development Project (CDP) – a series of small-scale local experiments 'aimed at finding new ways of meeting the needs of people living in areas of high social deprivation'.[16] Twelve projects were eventually established, each with a local action team backed by the research facilities of a university or polytechnic.

The projects were widely spread geographically and covered a variety of local situations. One was in the semi-rural parishes of an old mining and metal-working area, another in six South Wales coal-mining villages whose pits had closed. Two were in 1930s' council housing estates, two in declining textile towns, and three others in dockland areas of declining industry, 'redevelopment' and high unemployment. Despite local variations, all the projects soon turned up similar symptoms: residents with lower-than-average incomes, a disproportionately high rate of unemployment, high dependence on state benefits, poor health (sometimes including a high infant mortality rate), lack of basic amenities (baths, inside toilets, etc.), overcrowding, damp and dilapidated accommodati ,n, and the stigma of a bad reputation.

In the beginning it was assumed that the problems of poverty had two main causes. One was 'the characteristics of local populations' – in other words the personal inadequacy of individuals and families. They were, it was believed, small concentrations of families with special defects, caught up in a generation-to-generation cycle of poverty. A second and allied cause was thought to be the structural inadequacy of local government – poor planning, lack of communication with the public, and inadequate co-ordination of social services so that people slipped through the net. The task of the projects was, then, to bring the welfare services into touch with people who needed them, and to encourage self-help and mutual aid, 'even among those who experience most difficulty in standing on their own feet'.[17]

Working at first quite independently, the project teams discovered that such aims and explanations were inadequate. The Glamorgan project found that its area's problems were caused less by personal inadequacy than by changes in the South Wales coalfield and the ineffectiveness of regional policy.[18] The project team in Canning Town concluded that better organization of welfare services and help to families would only make a marginal difference to the problems of the area.[19] The Newcastle team also moved away from their initial assumptions about uncoordinated welfare services and the cycle of deprivation. 'Our experience at Benwell ... convinces us that such a definition of the local community's problems is inadequate, and that much of the disadvantage to be observed arises from structural causes', such as the changing nature and location of employment.[20]

Similarly, the first phase of the Coventry project showed that the distinctive feature of Hillfields – the protracted delay and decay of planning blight – was in no sense the fault of the local people. The persistence of poverty could not be explained by some breakdown of community, since informal networks of caring had survived and adapted remarkably well. Nor could it be said that poverty was caused by a concentration of problem people. 'In spite of its reputation, Hillfields did not have any abnormal share of deviant, apathetic or "inadequate" families ... Even where there were symptoms of stress and breakdown, these were often directly attributable to the pressures of living in poor housing or on inadequate incomes.' Few of the area's problems (except redevelopment) were different from those experienced by large sections of the population in other parts of the city, or in other parts of Britain. The particular burden carried by Hillfields was in their combination and concentration. Its poverty was not a stray microbe, but a microcosm of the wider society.[21]

With such mounting evidence, the twelve project teams compared notes, and issued a joint report. They concluded that the symptoms of poverty and deprivation they had encountered 'cannot be explained adequately by any abnormal preponderance of individuals or families whose behaviour could be defined as "pathological"'. The social malaise found in some areas was more a product of economic pressures than of personal inadequacies.[22] The belief that the poverty of whole areas is due to the inadequacy and inferiority of their inhabitants rather than the total structure of our society is a natural and comfortable conviction for the beneficiaries of injustice. The evidence, however, increasingly tells against it.

Similarly, the comfortable belief that apathy is the cause of poverty, rather than the result of the powerlessness of the poor, is not borne out by experience on either side of the Atlantic. In March 1966, Sargent Shriver spoke to the United States Congress about the effects of the Poverty Programme. 'The experts said the poor are apathetic, inarticulate, incapable of formulating demands, assisting and diagnosing their own needs. They were wrong. The poor are only waiting for the opportunity to be heard on a subject only they understand.' The overwhelming response to employment training and education programmes showed that apathy was not the key. The tragedy was that the available jobs were pitifully few, and that the marginal resources set aside for such programmes could not significantly increase them.[23]

In Britain, a Methodist minister concludes his discussion of the Hillfields project by attacking the common belief that deprived areas lack leadership. Though there is sometimes a lack of organizational skills, there is no lack of ability and potential. The problem is that people in the area 'have never before had a chance to participate in the exercise of power. Given opportunity, they can do it with judgment.' In Hillfields, 'more than twenty groups of various kinds are run and controlled by local people. Leaders have emerged. People have acquired new skills. "Clients" have become advocates. Inter-group conflicts of interests have been resolved. And all this has happened in an area which was written off by many people'.[24]

### *A natural complacence towards injustice*

Because they believe that the victims of an unjust and oppressive society are inferior, the beneficiaries of injustice cannot see them as individual persons of equal worth.[25] Some English tourists were being entertained on their first visit to Johannesburg by a well-established businessman. He was a thoughtful, likeable man, and a pillar of his church. After several years in South Africa, he was able to turn to his guests and off-handedly admit that he could not remember which waiter had served them. He looked round the restaurant, at the varied Indian, African and Coloured faces of the staff, and said, 'They're all alike to me'. Speaking of his white supervisor in the factory, a black worker said, 'He has an attitude of mind – this boy (sic) is black, therefore he will do this badly like the one before him. He has no critical eye to see who this person is'. 'If one African has made a mistake,' said another, 'automatically all Africans are liable to make the very same mistake. Yet with regard to whites, they judge their brother's case on its merits, and judge him as an individual.' Paradoxically, this attitude usually goes hand-in-hand with a claim to understand the oppressed group and to know what is best for them. 'We *know* the Bantu,' said the Afrikaans theology professor. 'We *know* the Coloureds. We're trying to help them, to see if they can do better. But we know you can't rush these things too.'

In a less dramatic way, British and American middle class people easily see the poorer members of their own society as an undifferentiated mass. 'They' are labelled as inadequates, social cripples, problem families, and scroungers on the state. Social distance from the daily experience of the victims of injustice, and the unreality of other people's needs compared with our own,[26] give the beneficiaries a 'natural complacence toward injustice'[27] which should always be treated with suspicion, especially within oneself. If I am a gainer rather than a loser, if I benefit from things as they are, and if change towards justice would for me be a change for the worse, I shall find it hard to understand those who want radical change now. I shall say – and probably half-believe – that things are not as bad as they seem. I shall hear and hear, but fear to understand. I shall see and see, yet lack the courage to act on what I see or accept the consequences of change.

# 7

# Awakening to Justice

Significant change occurs when people stop believing in what may once have been true, but has now become false; when they withdraw support from institutions which may once have served them but no longer do; when they refuse to submit to what may once have been fair terms but which are no longer. Such changes, when they occur, are the produce of true education.[1]

The old order ends, no matter what Bastilles remain, when the enslaved, within themselves, bury the psychology of servitude.

Martin Luther King

A black Methodist minister in South Africa was asked to explain that upsurge of assertiveness, artistic creativity and self-confidence among his people known as 'black consciousness'. 'It is beyond me to define in human words what it is,' he said. 'How do you put on paper the fact that you are awake?'[2]

Education for justice tries to assist an awakening. As suggested in a previous chapter, it is the birthright of every person to become not only self-conscious, but critically conscious. Critical consciousness is not an automatic development, but the product of true education. When people have been culturally oppressed, whether in the Latin American *latifundium* or the powerlessness of urban blight, the development of a critical consciousness is a first step towards freedom. It is action in the sphere of culture, which reverberates in the realms of economic and political power.[3]

Cultural oppression succeeds when the oppressor-beneficiary's belief that the victims of injustice are lazy, inferior, apathetic, inadequate, etc. is accepted by the latter. It follows that freedom from cultural oppression can only be achieved as people on both sides of the great divide eject such myths and act accordingly. In terms of Claudius Ceccon's cartoon, the black man has to square his shoulders, lift up his eyes, throw the image of the cigar-smoking boss out of his mind, and become a whole person, who does his thinking, seeing, planning and hoping for himself.

Justice demands that the method used to bring about such changes must avoid the cultural oppression it is trying to overcome. It cannot therefore be a transmission model of education, telling people what to believe. Nor can it be a propaganda exercise where people – oppressors or oppressed – are persuaded to exchange one set of slogans for another. As already indicated, it must be a method of dialogue which takes people seriously even when challenging their present beliefs.[4] It will therefore begin with people's own experience, seeing their situation in the family, at work, at school, and in their community as the springboard of understanding – though of course it will not end there. It will use codifications of the situation, and enabling or problem-posing questions, to reflect people's experience back to them in such a way that they can stand back from it and see it as an open problem for their investigation. In this way it will seek to develop, in both teacher-learner and learner-teachers, a critical consciousness which tacks constantly between theory and practice, action and reflection.[5] Paulo Freire calls this process *conscientization*. It is not an intellectual exercise, but a change of awareness which affects both reason and emotions, and learns by action as well as thought.

Though it is dialogue, not propaganda, conscientization (like any form of education) does not claim to be neutral or value-free. It begins its dialogue from definite values and beliefs. Because its political implications are radical it is worth recalling what some of these beliefs are. The person engaged in conscientization believes, for example, that social and economic inequalities ought to be arranged so that they are to the greatest benefit of the least advantaged members of society. She believes that natural inequalities of talent and skill should be treated as a common asset, not as a free-for-all for personal gain, and that the institutions and structures of society should demonstrate a respect for the dignity and worth of all its members. She treats other people, and believes that society ought to treat them, as knowing subjects with a right to find their voice. She assumes that even the most oppressed and 'inadequate' people already have knowledge and capabilities. She regards faith in people as a self-fulfilling prophecy. Thus, whenever and wherever a society falls short of these ideals, and wherever people accept beliefs which contradict them and help to perpetuate suffering and injustice, *she believes that it is both necessary and right to disturb them, as a first step towards change.* The aims and results of such disturbance-through-dialogue will however be different according to whether the people concerned are beneficiaries-oppressors or victims-oppressed.

## The awakening of the oppressed

One of the most subversive political statements ever uttered was the massed chant at black American civil rights meetings in the 1960s – 'I am somebody! Yes. Praise the Lord! I am somebody!' If I come to believe that I am 'somebody' – that I am not basically inferior to others – then I will no longer be able to believe that my poverty, bleak living conditions and low life chances are caused by my own failure as a person, by lack of moral fibre, or by apathy. I will see my previous passivity and apathy more as the result of poverty than its cause.

If the causes of poverty are not, by and large, in my own failure as a person, then they must lie in the structures of society. As I develop a critical consciousness I shall therefore try to understand these structures. I shall eject the myths of inferiority and inadequacy that others have implanted in me, and try to change my situation. The development of critical consciousness cannot therefore avoid having political implications. The changed awareness in the oppressed person will inevitably take a political shape and direction. The obvious alternative to saying 'I am inadequate' is to say 'I am being treated unjustly' or 'I am being oppressed'. 'They used to say we were unproductive because we were lazy and drunkards', said the member of the Chilean Agricultural Reform Unit. 'All lies. Now that we are respected as men, we're going to show everyone that we were never drunkards or lazy. We were exploited!'[6]

Similarly, though black consciousness in South Africa is a cultural phenomenon, the political implications of the following description do not need spelling out:

Black consciousness is the former Kaffir, Hottentot, Coolie, Non-European, Bantu and Non-white saying loudly 'NO' to the Baas, the Master, the European and the White. It is the Black man saying NO to White racism in all its forms ... No more is he going to try and fit into a non-white's portrait drawn by the white man. No more is he going to say what the white man wants to hear and thus continue his own indignity. No more does the white man epitomise all that is good, just and of value. No more is the white man the black man's yardstick of humanity.[7]

In Britain, too, the logical alternative to inferiority, inadequacy and lack of communication as adequate explanations of poverty is to look at the total framework of our society. When experience of working with people in several different areas led the CDP teams to reject the first explanation, they naturally moved towards the second. 'The project reports demonstrate that the decline of working class areas is an inevitable consequence of this external economic process which has led locally to different forms of withdrawal and reinvestment of capital.' The only way to alter the situation is to bring about a fundamental change in the distribution of wealth and power in society as a whole. The proper strategy for a programme like CDP is therefore 'to work with local people in generating a political awareness of these processes, and support action which works towards change: *in short a political education programme.*'[8]

The type of political action that results from such education will vary from country to country, and even from town to town. Every group engaged in it will have to make the classic choices of tactics and principle – consensus or conflict, court actions or civil disobedience, debates or boycotts, violent or non-violent action. The likely range of such choices in a society like ours will be considered more fully in the next chapter. Meanwhile, two general points may be made.

Firstly, in political awakening and action, great oaks from little acorns grow. Before people can gain the strength to fight together for something, they need not only the conviction that they are right, and that they can win, but also 'activities and organizations that help their day-to-day lives in order to have the strength to fight against the odds over the months'. In one area of London, a single playgroup on a shoe-string budget sparked off a network of other playgroups and a long-term playspace campaign. Then, as people worked together, and made contact with each other, the common problem of housing conditions kept coming up in discussion. This led first to the formation of a Housing Advice Centre, and then to a series of campaigns against encroaching traffic schemes, the slowness of the local council, and the incursions of property developers.[9] Similarly, the CDP teams have assisted in setting up community law centres, housing advice centres, pre-school education work, adventure playgrounds, adult education courses, and old people's welfare schemes, while also researching into employment, industrial investment, housing, and welfare rights – believing that such activities can be the seeds of a broader political awakening.

Secondly, the victims of injustice do not, by definition, have much cultural, economic or political power, except, sometimes, the near-empty formality of the vote. Their main asset – often their only asset – is in their numbers and unity. 'It is axiomatic to the political scientist that people, unorganised, are virtually powerless. Solutions to the problems of poverty ... must come through organised efforts ... solutions which are most appropriate to the people must involve organisation of the people affected by them.'[10] The aim of conscientization must therefore be for the victims of injustice to see themselves as an oppressed *group*. It must not encourage individuals to migrate out of poverty up the slim ladders of individual success which serve to defuse unrest and postpone fundamental change. The idea of the 'ladder of opportunity' is deeply ingrained in Western societies. The problem is that, by definition, only the individual can climb it. The unspoken assumption is that most people are doomed to remain below. Justice can only be established when the victims of injustice realize that such ladders are a delusion, and that other people's problems are part of their own.

## The awakening of oppressors

Education for justice seeks to make the victims of injustice aware of their position as a group, so that they can unite and work for change. The position of the oppressor-beneficiary is different. Because groups and classes in society never surrender power without conflict, and because the whole group cannot reasonably be expected to become loving and moral,[11] the beneficiaries of injustice must be seen and approached *as individuals*. Only a few can be expected to respond, to awaken to their position and act positively for change.[12] I shall therefore look at some of the main obstacles to such an awakening, and the main kinds of action which the awakened beneficiary-oppressor can take, either as an individual, or with the few others likely to join him.

Many victims, and most beneficiaries of injustice become frightened, angry, or bewildered when anyone starts talking about justice, domination, oppression, freedom and power. Middle class people can react with astonishing fear and hostility to the suggestion that poverty in Birmingham, Glasgow, London, Africa or Asia might be causally related to their own comfortable living standards and assured social position. For convenience, the person who raises such questions will be called 'the educator' (whatever his or her actual profession may be). What follows also applies, of course, to the *self-educator* – the person who is coming to terms with such questions within herself.

The first point for the educator to recognize is that such feelings of hostility, disturbance and rejection are inevitable. They cannot be bypassed, but must be faced and understood – in oneself and in others. Conflict cannot be avoided – and that includes inner conflict. Hostility and fear are painful to all concerned, the educator included, for it is not easy to raise such questions against a hostile reaction. Yet dialogue education will not react to hostility with polemic or counter-anger. It will not try to batter people with facts (though factual knowledge is important). Instead, it will try to see the hostility and fear itself as a problem. It will ask, '*Why* is there this hostility (in the group or in myself)? Why is the reaction more than merely intellectual? How can such feelings be examined and understood? How can we work through them, come to terms with them, and investigate the issues in a less emotional way?'.

A second likely reaction is guilt, whether open or suppressed. Two equally unhelpful responses are to wallow in it or reject it. On the one hand, it is pointless to take the sins of our slave-dealing forbears on our own shoulders and sit paralysed in sackcloth and ashes. On the other hand, studies in post-war Germany suggest that apathy and indifference towards injustice may well be due to an unwillingness to admit and come to terms with it, to an 'inability to grieve'.[13]

As with hostility, the guilt of the awakening oppressor must be treated as a problem, in this case one of self-acceptance. During a visit to the United States, Freire was struck by the number of liberal whites who would sit silent, with heads bowed, during discussions with blacks, or who spoke deferentially, hesitantly, as if afraid to criticize. Perhaps, he surmised, they had not yet come to terms with guilt, *and could not accept themselves as white.*

Such self-acceptance is the key to personal change. For the Christian, it means going back to the gospel promise of love that accepts all, without distinction – just and unjust, black and white, poor and rich, the oppressed and their oppressors. This insight lay behind the attempt by members of the Christian Institute of Southern Africa to create a 'white consciousness' among their fellow English-speakers and Afrikaaners. White consciousness meant, first of all, seeing and admitting one's involvement in the oppressive system. 'The first thing we must do is to become alive to the fact that we are the oppressors – not Mr Vorster, not the government, nor even the Nationalists, but "we, the accused". The government could not survive without the acquiescence and support of the large majority of the whites.'[14]

In similar terms, the person who awakens to find herself a middle class beneficiary of institutions which perpetuate poverty at home and overseas, must first recognize that 'we are the oppressors'. Yet having done that, it is essential to accept oneself *as* white, British, middle class or whatever – to see the positive features in our nationality, colour and social position so that we can work constructively for change:

> *We do not seek to live in guilt, nor do we want to apologise for our being.* We are white (or it may be, British, prosperous, articulate, or middle-class) and are aware of it and that is a given and cannot be changed. We are, however, bent on finding a way to cope with injustice, from a position of strength, not weakness, and from a sense of ourselves that is positive, not negative.[15]

A third likely reaction in the awakening oppressor is bafflement. Whenever I meet a group of people in Britain who are concerned about world poverty and injustice, their insistent question is, 'But what can we *do*?' On the surface, this is simply a request for information, for a list of ideas for action. But the tone of voice usually indicates a deeper psychological question – 'What *can* we do?' People ask the question so insistently, not because they lack knowledge or imagination, but because they feel baffled, frustrated and overwhelmed – by the scale of human suffering, by the maze of economics, and by the lack of obvious targets or of action that can bring quick results. The certainty that they *are* involved and responsible joins in a paralysing embrace with the conviction that as housewives, clerks, desk-bound executives, classroom-bound teachers, harrassed clergy, or old age pensioners their action cannot make any significant difference.

The first response to bafflement should not be to hand out a list of possible activities, but to ask whether the uncertainty and bewilderment can be understood in a positive way. Bafflement and frustration are often a necessary stage in personal growth. To retreat from them into either busy-ness or inactivity is to miss the chance of new discovery. The person who accepts bafflement and continues to wrestle with it and question himself in a spirit of hope will sooner or later find a new understanding and sense of direction.[16] In my experience, *everyone* has some choice they can make, some simple step towards justice. Once the first step has been taken, commitment is self-reinforcing. A suburban house-wife turns her front room into a Third World Education Centre and lends material to local schools. Solicitors give part time advice at Law Centres. Retired trade unionists find that their organizing skills can be of use to tenants associations or their fellow-pensioners. Housebound people monitor the newspapers and collect press cuttings for world development action groups. Families choose a simpler life-style. Men and women change career in middle life, while students look at their career prospects in a new light.

### *Identification or erosion?*

Dialogue forbids one person to prescribe what others should do and the variety of individual situations fortunately makes it impossible. But for the beneficiary of injustice who has some range of choice, there are two main forms of action. One is *identification*, a radical change which entails leaving one's privileged position and joining with people or groups who are in some way oppressed – for example, by moving into the inner city and accepting its problems, or by working for a time overseas.

Identification usually involves a hard inner struggle to overcome one's own arrogance or desire to assume leadership. It is a training in humility, in recognizing one's own limitations – including the fact that the cultural and economic advantages which make identification possible also give their owner a built-in return ticket to his own country, or to the suburbs, if the pressure grows too great. To accept such limitations honestly can, however, make identification a powerful witness to one's fellow oppressors. In 1972, the parish priest of Dimbaza, David Russell, lived for six months on the five-rand-a-month pension of his older, black parishioners, to try and bring home to his fellow whites the suffering of 'resettled' African people (the amount, about £4 in 1975 English values, allows only a starvation diet). He experienced lassitude and apathy, a slowing down of mind and body often dismissed as laziness by well-fed whites. At the end of his fast he wrote an open letter to other clergy and ministers, and said, 'Tomorrow I will be free to live normally again ... I feel brittle and wrung out. I have a great longing and need for a break from it all, like a man about to be released from prison. *For most of our Black brothers in Christ, however, there is no release. For too many the situation is intolerable, humiliating, unending.*'[17]

The other option for the conscientized oppressor is *erosion* – a sustained attempt to chip away at the foundations of cultural, economic and political power that perpetuate injustice, and to do so quietly, from the inside. If conflict is inevitable, and the beneficiaries of injustice will not make concessions without demand, the proper course is not to run away from these unpleasant realities, but to weaken the oppressors' resistance to change or try to ease and channel the conflict when it comes.

In cultural terms, erosion means taking every opportunity of exposing the myths, fixed ideas and pretensions of the oppressor groups to which one belongs. This is a patient, determined debunking, not shrill or bitter, but loving, forceful, even humorous and ironical. 'When power is robbed of the shining armor of political, moral and philosophical theories, by which it defends itself it will fight on without armor; but it will be more vulnerable, and the strength of its enemies is increased.'[18] The cultural sapper takes his dynamite sticks of poems, cartoons, case studies, metaphors, statistics, academic expertise or personal-experience-stories and explodes them at key points under the myths that the victims of injustice are lazy, inadequate or inferior. If he cannot join the victims he can at least try to make his own group more willing to talk than to shoot, more likely to bargain and make concessions than unleash the full force of their political and economic power. If he has some professional expertise or special knowledge, he can put it at the disposal of others, or use it to question the assumptions of the powers that be.

Such programmes of erosion face two dangers. One is compromise. It is hard to go on being one of the few people in one's social circle, family or workplace who goes against the stream. Without the support of even a few others, the persistent worker for cultural, political or economic erosion is easily written off as a hobby-horse rider. Or else, as pressures mount, her effort loses its sharpness and she falls back on ineffective gestures – putting every effort, as someone has said, into rearranging deck-chairs on the Titanic.

The other pitfall is haphazardness. Without a clear understanding of the task and a definite programme of action, the cultural sapper ends up making firework displays rather than controlled explosions. Or he forgets that he is trying to open the way to fundamental change, and falls back on uncoordinated acts of charity. Ultimately, the only way to remain effective is to work with others, follow a definite aim and strategy, and be honest in assessing its results. Even soup kitchens can give people enough warmth in their bellies to discover their potential and rebel against injustice – but everything depends on their placing and timing. It is not enough to make gallons of Mrs Beeton's charity soup and dish it out at random.

Conscientization, says Paulo Freire, is a painful birth. It means dying to cherished myths and false securities, and coming alive to critical awareness and hopeful action. 'As I conscientize myself I realize that my brothers who don't eat, who don't laugh, who don't sing, who don't love, who live oppressed, crushed and despised, are suffering all this because of some reality that is causing it. And at that point I join in the action historically by genuinely loving, by having the courage to commit myself. Or I end up with a sense of guilt because I am not doing what I know I should.' If I stop being naive about my place in an unjust society, and my personal involvement in other people's suffering and oppression, then I must either become shrewdly cynical and cling doggedly to what I have, or become radical, working for justice and accepting the cost and risks involved.

What I cannot do is to go back to my former ignorance, and find peace through philanthropy or good works. For 'peace cannot be purchased. It is not for sale. Peace has to be lived. There is only one way to find peace: to work for it, shoulder to shoulder with my fellow-men.'[19]

# 8

# Learning the Realities of Power

Governments, like the authorities in universities, have a siege mentality: if only they can hold out long enough, they can hope that the pressuring groups will disappear or change.                                    John Dearlove

We do not intend participating in our poverty.
We intend organising to abolish it.
East London Claimants Union[1]

In April 1963 Dr Martin Luther King wrote a letter from his prison cell in Birmingham, Alabama, to a group of white clergy who had publicly attacked his methods of protest against racial segregation. He confessed his disappointment with moderate whites who preferred 'a negative peace which is the absence of tension to a positive peace which is the presence of justice'. Their criticism of the civil rights movement was based on the false assumption that it was creating conflict. In fact, the movement was merely bringing to the surface the hidden tension caused by years of oppression and discrimination. 'Like a boil that can never be cured so long as it is covered up, but must be opened with all its ugliness to the natural medicines of air and light, injustice must be exposed, with all the tension its exposure creates, to the light of human conscience and the air of national opinion before it can be cured.'[2]

In an earlier chapter I argued that social justice can only be established through conflicts in which we must often take sides and work with some people against others.[3] To do this effectively, we have to be, in another phrase of Martin Luther King's, tough-minded and tenderhearted. Tough-mindedness is needed to understand the realities of power, the tactics of the powerful and how to oppose them, and the necessity, sometimes, of bringing hidden tensions to the surface. Tenderheartedness is needed to enter the conflict wholeheartedly yet without hate and to use methods which are most likely, in the end, to bring about the positive peace that is the presence of justice.

## *Levels of conflict*

In Western industrial societies there seem to be four possible levels of conflict in any situation of injustice.[4] At the lowest level, a housing action group approaches the local council about the plight of homeless families and meets the response, 'We agree that these families are the council's responsibility and that they must be rehoused. The problem is how and where.' The reply means that there is a *consensus* or agreement as to what the problem is. Any differences between the action group and the council are based solely on misinformation or lack of communication. All that is needed is a rational approach based on goodwill. Appropriate tactics will include information-gathering, joint working parties, and attempts to inform the general public.

The second level of conflict is where the local council is unwilling to accept responsibility for housing the people in question. There is then a *difference* of opinion about the problem, based not merely on misinformation but also on such factors as vested interests and emotional resistance – like the councillor who declares that there *can't* be any slums in his ward. Where resistance from the power-holders is irrational, reasoned discussion and better communication will not be enough to change their point of view. The housing group will need, not only study and debate, but a campaign to arouse public opinion and bring other sources of power to bear so that the councillors are obliged to act on the information put before them. Tactics will include public meetings, petitions, letter-writing campaigns, and the mild coercion of press publicity and public reaction. The aim will be to bring the issue up the scale of priorities so that it gets a higher place on the council's agenda.

When the authority categorically refuses to discuss an issue or accept responsibility – even in spite of the type of campaign described above – there is a more serious level of conflict which can be described as *dissensus*. The number needing to be rehoused is probably quite large – say a whole area of the town – and the council may be intransigent because to accept responsibility would mean a complete change of policy. The action group will then have two choices. It can give up, or contest the issue. Research and campaigning will probably then be supplemented by protest and disruption. Broadly speaking, such tactics are of three kinds: firstly, clashes that stay within the accepted rules of behaviour (e.g. court actions and other legal procedures); secondly, clashes that break social conventions and cause disturbance without breaking the law (e.g. demonstrations, marches, boycotts, rent strikes, renouncing honours, silent vigils, and 'haunting' representatives of authority by peacefully following and watching them); and thirdly, clashes that break the law in a controlled and disciplined way, where the protestors are willing to accept the consequences of their action (e.g. tax refusal and civil disobedience).[5]

The ultimate level of conflict – unlikely over a housing issue – is *insurrection*. It differs from the other three not merely in degree but in kind. In consensus, difference and dissensus all the parties accept that the powers that be (e.g. local councils) have at least some moral claim to their authority. The protestors' aim is to persuade the authorities to do their job properly and fulfil their responsibilities. Even civil disobedience appeals to what the law *ought* to be and assumes that the changes demanded can be made by the present social order. Insurrection occurs, however, when the opposition group believes, rightly or wrongly, that the authorities have forfeited their right to rule, and must be challenged and overthrown. The difference between dissensus and insurrection is particularly important, and needs to be clearly understood by all concerned.

Before moving on, two comments may be made. Firstly, Western industrial societies place great value on consensus – so much so that many people are apt to see consensus when it is not there. They prefer 'cooperation, no matter how spurious, to conflict, no matter how necessary.'[6] For twelve months, local residents' groups in a Midlands town negotiated with the council about the problems of derelict houses. They wrote letters to council departments and ward councillors, held public meetings and took the local MP on a walkabout. A community development team documented the problem, convened an interdepartmental working group, submitted reports to the chief officer's board, and had meetings with officials both locally and in Whitehall. There was no visible improvement, and the council said its hands were tied.

Then one night, a child got stuck on the roof of a derelict house. Next day, angry mothers stormed into the town hall and interrupted the council meeting. They were ejected, but the television and press publicity got immediate results. The council somehow discovered that it *could* act, and had the houses boarded up.[7] Such examples could be multiplied a hundredfold. They suggest that the toughminded worker for justice will have a healthy scepticism of consensus interpretations.

Secondly, the most powerful pressure-tactics should go hand-in-hand with attempts to understand the conflict and open the way to negotiation. The aim of the worker for justice must be to pull a situation back from dissensus to difference, and eventually arrive at a consensus. Sometimes this can be done by looking beneath the surface aims of the opposing groups. If their aims are rational, it is often possible to find common ground at a deeper level. If A wants the window open and B wants it shut, there is an irreconcilable conflict. If A's deeper goal is fresh air and B wants to avoid the direct north wind, it may be possible for them to reach agreement on a ventilation system that will satisfy both – provided, of course, that A and B respect each other's aims and are bargaining on equal terms.

### The tactics of the powerful

Besides being able to see different levels of conflict, and the tactics appropriate for each, the worker for justice also needs to know the tactics of power – the various devices which authority down the ages has used to fend off pressure for radical change.

At the lowest level of conflict, authority uses the tactic of *enlistment*. When voluntary bodies or pressure groups raise their voice about an issue, authority responds by saying, in effect, 'Prove your sincerity by doing something practical yourself. Moderate your demands to a more acceptable level, set up a voluntary scheme, and work with us to tackle the problem.' If entered into with open eyes and adequate safeguards such partnerships may well serve the cause of justice. But they may also rob the voluntary body of its cutting edge and financial independence. A council of social service which moves from pressure campaigns about housing conditions to forming a housing association may help several homeless families – but it will forfeit any claim to be tackling the causes of homelessness. Because of its apparent reasonableness, the tactic of enlistment often succeeds in heading off criticism.

If the opposition cannot be enlisted, the next obvious tactic is *delay*. 'We ought to discuss this as widely as possible', 'We must consult very widely before moving to a decision', 'We agree in principle but the money just isn't available', 'There are so many groups involved – we should *co-ordinate* all these different efforts and establish a joint committee' – these are some of the bureaucrat's instinctive reactions to a difficult or controversial suggestion. The effect, or even hope, is that if decisions are delayed for long enough, the protesting group will run out of steam, turn its energies elsewhere, or tone down its demands.

In practice, of course, consultation can be infinitely wide, while co-ordination results in a Tibetan prayer wheel of joint committees where everyone dissipates their energy by endlessly meeting everyone else. The antidote to delay is to add pressure tactics to reasoned debate, and to refuse consultation and co-ordination which do not carry an effective slice of power.

A third classic ploy is *divide and rule*. Like all the tactics of power, it is a natural reaction of authority, and does not *necessarily* spring from conscious manipulation or Machiavellian cunning. The head of a large charity once announced that he would negotiate only with one staff body – the trade union branch or the internal staff association – and told the staff members to choose between them. It was a reasonable request in itself, but the effect was to foster a division of loyalties, and hinder the unity – and therefore the potential influence – of the staff as a whole. Despite the reasonableness of such tactics from the authorities' point of view, they should be patiently and forcefully resisted.

A fourth tactic is *conciliation* – a premature appeal to all the parties in a dispute to sink their differences and sit together round a table. When the conflict has been faced and brought into the open, and when the parties seek agreement on the basis of equal strength, such an appeal should be heeded. Frequently, however, the appeal is made in order to *avoid* conflict, fudge the issues, or put the opposition on the wrong foot and persuade it to fillet the backbone out of its demands.

If the opposition persists in its campaign, and remains vigorous and united, another tactic is *cooptation*[8] (often called 'participation'). Cooptation means, for example, inviting parents to elect some of their number to a management committee, or asking citizens' groups to appoint representatives to a joint committee discussing plans for a new estate. Cooptation is a much more positive response than those previously noted. It recognizes that people can only affect a decision if they have a voice and a vote at the point where the decision is taken. It gives power-holders the opportunity to hear an alternative viewpoint at first hand, and so modify their policies.

Yet cooptation has serious limitations. If justice can only be established by equal power, it is unlikely that a token or minority representation will greatly alter the cut of committee decisions – except by trimming the edges and making minor adjustments to the seams. In Newcastle-upon-Tyne an advisory committee of councillors, officials and citizens met to discuss plans for the Rye Hill area of the city. One citizen commented as follows: 'It's like going home and your wife says, "Would you like bacon and eggs for tea?", and you say, 'No, I'd like steak and chips", and you end up with bacon and eggs – she listens to what you say, but it's still bacon and eggs.'[9]

Because cooptation gives the appearance of power without the substance it may confuse people and weaken their determination to keep pressing for change. Yet cooptation should not necessarily be refused. If people are offered a token share of power at the price of co-operation and acquiescence, 'they will be shrewd to take the power but refuse the co-operation, exploiting each concession to demand more.'[10] Participation is valuable provided that it gives an *effective* voice in decisions. But if you are invited to contribute to a plan, and find that it is vaguely stated, that all and sundry are invited to contribute, that the planners do not control its finance and administration, and that the timetable for decisions is totally unrelated to the progress of consultation, then the 'participation' is unlikely to mean much, and the plan will probably come to nothing.[11]

A final tactic worth noting is *diversion*. The powers that be, the ruling groups in society, almost always convince themselves that their interests are those of society as a whole. They therefore meet opposition by pointing to their legal authority. They try to divert attention from the issue being presented to the competence of the opposition, or the way in which it is pressing its claim.

At lower levels of conflict, diversion appears as, 'If only you'd go through the proper channels', a response which ignores the power of vested interests and assumes that the problem is merely one of communication. In a situation of dissensus, the power holders try to put their challengers at a moral disadvantage by attacking their methods. Outcries about squatting or picketing often divert public attention away from the housing problem or the grievance behind a strike. In 1965, some men moved into the King Hill Hostel for homeless families, to protest against the rule that forbade them to live there with their wives and children. During the long battle that followed the authorities constantly tried to divert attention from the real issue by branding campaign activists who were not themselves homeless as politically motivated troublemakers.

### Solidarity, partisanship and truth

The awakening of the victims of injustice must lead to their organization and action as a group. Numbers and unity are their main strength, and group solidarity is essential if the tactics of delay, divide-and-rule, cooptation and diversion are to be successfully resisted. To join in a struggle for justice on a particular issue means taking sides and working *with* some people *against* others. As indicated earlier, there is a dialectical tension between outrageous partisanship for the poor and oppressed and a devotion to the claims of love and truth.

In considering this tension we must first accept that partisanship and one-sidedness cannot be avoided in any effective struggle for justice. To show genuine interest and identification means allowing people to define the problems they see themselves facing. Working class people, for example, will probably see their problems in a very different way from welfare authorities and the town hall. Thus, if they are alienated from the education system because it does not reflect their interests and meet their needs, the educationist must enter into a dialogue 'from a position of solidarity with them, so that they may interpret their social situation, and the actions they take, in the light of their own values and interests'.[12]

Perhaps the greatest mental obstacle to wholehearted solidarity is the lingering belief that somewhere there is an objective truth about a situation which can be discovered and accepted by all. This is rarely the case in the initial stages of serious social conflict.

Suppose, for example, that a family is on a holiday outing. They stop the car at a crossroads, uncertain of their direction. If everyone is agreed about their destination, more information will help them to find the way.

Perhaps, however, the family has not yet agreed what the destination should be – because different members have different interests. Some are for the beach, others are for the mountains. The parents want to laze in the sun, while the teenage daughter wants to dance in the discotheque. If they discuss where to go next, information now has partisan implications, however accurate it may be: rain is forecast – the map shows a scenic road – the radio reports that roads to the beach are jammed with traffic – the discotheque is just around the corner – but there is nowhere to park the car. All these facts are relevant, but the weight of each item is controversial. The voice from the back seat pointing out an ice cream van may be pointedly ignored. There is at once too much information and too little. The ultimate question – what the party as a whole will enjoy – is unanswerable, and the amount of information on every possible choice is unmanageable.

It follows that as these holiday-makers discuss their route, 'they . . . will react to the advocacy implicit in the information each puts forward, *and priority of attention will go to the members of the party whose interests are dominant.* The same is surely true of the policymakers: information is prejudicial, competitive, inexhaustible and ultimately indeterminate.'[13]

This does not mean that the search for truth should be abandoned, or that we should deliberately select or distort information to suit our point of view. As the example indicates, the crucial question is not, 'what information is true?', but 'which information is relevant?'. 'It is not enough simply to present better information; you must also secure attention to it.'[14]

The control of information is one of the strongest weapons in the hands of people in power. Yet a society like ours has ample alternative sources for anyone who cares to look hard enough. The middle-class reader of mainstream newspapers who looks at some of the alternatives will be surprised to find new and unsuspected information about our society – much of it accurate and penetrating – which it would not pay his commercial newspaper to print.[15]

### *Conflict and reconciliation*

The requirements of unity and solidarity also help to explain why some oppressed groups feel that they must break off relations with moderate sympathizers in order to establish their own strength and identity: 'We shall earn the right to love all men by struggling against some; we shall earn the right to hold hands with all men by refusing to hold hands with all men who stand in the way of all men holding hands with all men.'[16] Such separation may not be sought for the sake of division, but to pave the way for genuine equality. 'In the temporary separation the black seeks to find his own identity and come back into unity a free man – so that it is one freedom uniting with another ... (But) we must unite as equals. A man must talk to a man.'[17]

Here lies the difference between conciliation and reconciliation. To people brought up in a well-ordered middle-class community, calls for struggle, solidarity and separation may seem puzzling and alarming. Their experience of conflict is likely to be of mild disputes which can easily be settled by reason and goodwill, and they are apt to apply this experience uncritically to the deeper divisions of society.

Such realities ought to be less shocking to Christian faith. For the good news of reconciliation between God and humanity is of a unity achieved at great cost, through suffering, toil – *and conflict*. 'When God reconciled us to himself he did not do that by smoothing over the history of our estrangement. In Christ, God organized the conflict: he showed man's rebellion for what it is.'[18] Jesus provoked the final conflict of his life by going to Jerusalem and confronting the religious-political authorities. His death on the cross shows the full extent of the conflict between good and evil, justice and injustice, love and hate. The power and surprise of the cross is not that it avoids conflict, but that out of weakness, failure, rejection and death it brings life, hope, purpose, and the opportunity for repentance and a new start.

In Christian experience, this reconciliation can be found here and now, as slaves and masters, oppressed and oppressors, intellectuals and workers learn to love and accept each other through their common faith in Jesus Christ. But it is not achieved lightly. In March 1973 I sat in on a board meeting of the Christian Institute of Southern Africa, in Johannesburg. The Board consisted of some thirty people, both black and white. The Christian Institute staff, and possibly other board members, were expecting an imminent subpoena to appear before the Schlebusch Commission, a government body 'investigating' several South African organizations.

Previously, the Board of the Christian Institute had taken the view that members should appear and testify before the Commission because they had nothing to hide – it was standard CI practice to give a free bunch of office keys to the Security Branch (State Security Police). Recent events had shown that the Schlebusch Commission was not an impartial inquiry. Hearings were held in secret. Witnesses subpoenaed to appear before the Commission could not be legally represented, nor cross-examine their questioners, nor know the evidence or charges against them. Some white members of the Board felt that the proper Christian response was to expose the government's hypocrisy by taking the initiative and publicly refusing to testify. They therefore proposed this to the meeting.

The board members knew each other well, and many were personal friends. Yet the proposal met with resistance or blank opposition, much of it muted or silent.

Gradually, it emerged that the proposers had overlooked the difference in the situation for white and black members. A bold decision would cause far more suffering or danger to black members than to white. It was impossible, in that society, for equal partners in Christ to be equal partners in suffering. It was psychologically easier for whites to contemplate boldness than for blacks.

When this hidden conflict came to light, the board was able to reach a common mind. A corporate decision not to testify would expose black members too strongly to intimidation. It was therefore resolved to give full support to any board members or staff who made individual decisions to this effect. There was unspoken knowledge that many of them would, but no dishonour on those who could not.

When the decision was reached, there was a deep sense of unity, a meeting across the terrible gulf of racial and economic oppression. It was, perhaps, an anticipation of what race-relationships in South Africa will one day be like. But it was not – and could not be – an assured possession. It was a treasure grasped for a moment, a miracle and a gift. It was worlds away from the agreeable like-mindedness of English Christianity, and from our easy talk of conciliation.

### The tactics of disruption

In our society, where conflict usually falls short of insurrection, a serious campaign for justice on a particular issue will nonetheless reach, very often, a situation of dissensus. The tactics of dissensus include squatting in unoccupied property, obstruction of the highway, interruptions of public events and occupation of public buildings. Because they are disturbing and conflictual it is worth considering their aims and methods from the viewpoint of social justice.

Martin Luther King's desegregation campaign in Birmingham, Alabama, went through four stages. It began with a careful collection of facts to determine the existence and extent of racial injustice. The second step was negotiation – but the city fathers adamantly refused to negotiate in good faith. The third step was self-purification, an education of the black community in the theory and practice of non-violent direct action. Training sessions were held for potential demonstrators. They were taught to expect harsh language and physical abuse, and to accept it without retaliation – 'to be cursed and not reply, to be beaten and not hit back'. All volunteers had to sign a commitment card pledging themselves to walk and talk in the manner of love, to show courtesy to friend and foe, to refrain from violence of fist, tongue or heart, and to follow the direction of the Movement, or of the leaders of a particular demonstration.

The final step was direct action – sit-ins at segregated lunch counters, marches into forbidden areas, and disregard of a delaying-action court order. Thousands went to jail, but in spite of rough handling, water cannon and police dogs the movement remained disruptive yet non-violent, and eventually won a considerable improvement in civil rights.[19]

The Birmingham campaign is a classic example of disruptive tactics in a situation of dissensus. Disruption is appropriate when, as in Birmingham, there is a grave injustice which needs to be set right; when negotiation and lawful protest have been tried and failed; when the disruption is carried out openly and selflessly, with foresight and acceptance of the consequences, including punishment; and when it violates orderly behaviour and breaks the law in order to appeal to what law ought to be. The aim of disruption is not merely to make a protest, but to move the other party towards negotiation. Because justice cannot be achieved without a better balance of power, direct action aims to make the protestors a force to be reckoned with. *It intends, not to harm but to hinder – to prevent the target system from operating, not to destroy it.*

Disruptive tactics face three major problems. Firstly, as in any inter-group conflict, innocent individuals on both sides will suffer with the rest. This cannot be avoided: even a boycott can threaten livelihoods or even life. It can only be minimized as far as possible. Secondly, disruption allows the governing authorities to use the tactic of diversion, and cry horror at the methods in order to avoid taking notice of the cause. Thirdly, even non-violent disruption may generate a violent reaction.

As our own recent history shows, disruption is not always or necessarily non-violent. Yet to avoid or minimize the above problems, non-violence should be maintained wherever possible. Non-violent pressure requires a discipline that is both spiritual and technical. The person who works for justice by such means must train herself inwardly to overcome the fear of physical violence, to maintain determination against threats, and to accept violent opposition without retaliation. Technical training includes the organization and control of parades, vigils, sit-ins etc., and the mastery of physical techniques like falling lightly when attacked, going limp on arrest, and linking arms in a crowd. Non-violent action will involve casualties, sometimes heavy casualties, though they are unlikely to be as heavy as those arising out of violent action.[20]

Despite the possible costs, non-violent techniques have several advantages. They can be used effectively by people who are otherwise poor and weak. They give dignity to the users and rob the oppressive forces of their moral advantage. They combat injustice forcefully, yet without hate. Finally, they make justice visible in their methods, by seeking to include the oppressor or enemy in the eventual solution and reconciliation.

# 9

# Taking a Political Stand

> Ideological systems are needed for making sense of our experience,
> but they must be regarded with a certain suspicion.
>
> Alan Booth[1]

A political ideology is a mixture of beliefs, ideas and attitudes. It asks how a society actually works, and what it could become. These are not technical questions with a single clear-cut answer. If a car packs up on a country road, the mechanically minded motorist can get out the repair manual and work through the check list of possible faults, from dirty spark plugs to a cracked cylinder head. The questions, 'what is wrong and what needs to be done?' can be precisely answered, because the workings of the engine are precisely known.

A society is infinitely more complex than the internal combustion engine. Because our knowledge is incomplete, and biased by economic or political interests, the motorist's questions can only be answered provisionally, by developing a theory of how society works, and testing it out in action.

Many people, of course, do not use political ideologies in this way. They simply assume that their way of seeing society, their particular set of slogans ('free enterprise', 'equality of opportunity', 'common ownership of the means of production and exchange' etc.) is self-evidently true. To develop critical consciousness, however, means seeing our ideology as a *working hypothesis* which must be continually modified through action and reflection. An engineer once developed a mathematical model for a local water authority. The officials were delighted because the model made sense of several oddities in water-supply which they had previously been unable to predict or explain. When they used it in forward planning, their plans worked smoothly and the oddities disappeared. 'They were more enthusiastic about it than I was,' said the engineer, 'because I know the limitations of mathematical models. They accepted it because it worked so well in practice, and made sense of what they knew.' A sound ideology makes sense of past experience, connects different parts of our knowledge, and enables us to plan ahead with more confidence. But it is a model, not absolute truth, and should always be open to questioning and change.

Anyone who works for justice needs such an ideology, however local their work may be. Without a down-to-earth effort for justice, the wider vision becomes fooled by its own rhetoric and detached from reality. Without a coherent ideology the hard slog on particular issues will lose conviction or direction. It may achieve limited success in one area, but end up shifting the problem elsewhere. Or it may come up against larger problems which it cannot understand or deal with. To aim at 'community control' of neighbourhood politics while neglecting the deployment of industry and investment is like controlling the fleas in a circus while allowing the elephants to roam free.[2] Direct action on local grievances helps people to gain marginal improvements in their situation, and considerable improvements in their self-respect. But it is no substitute for a national approach and a more broadly based movement for political change.[3]

### The 'conservative' view – individual freedom and capitalist economics

The understanding of justice, power and conflict arrived at in earlier chapters rules out two of the most common political attitudes in Western industrial society.

It rules out, first of all, the right-wing ideology which places almost all its emphasis on the freedom of the individual. For simplicity, I shall call this ideology 'conservative', meaning not the detailed policies of the British Conservative Party or its counterparts elsewhere, but a basic attitude found both in and outside them.

Conservative ideology usually accepts the first principle of social justice, the principle of equal liberty. But it is wedded to an economic system – modified capitalism – which necessarily excludes the others. Because it depends on competitiveness, it sets people against each other, and so can do no more than verbal homage to mutual respect and a fundamental equality of worth. It respects the individual freedom of those who 'succeed' only by neglecting the freedom of those who 'fail'. In affluent societies it gives some protection to the poor and weak but not internationally. British and American firms which give tolerable rewards to workers in their own country are regularly found to pay starvation wages to their tea-pickers, copper miners or factory workers abroad, or to acquiesce with only minor modifications in the economic and racial horror of *apartheid*.[4] In commercial terms, *they have to*: moral indignation can do very little against the internal logic of the system. Ultimately, capitalist economics can give little place to human values. 'When it must choose between capital and man it will always choose capital.'[5]

Because of its inbuilt alliance with the free-for-all competitiveness of capitalism, the conservative ideology, unlike its aristocratic ancestors, cannot see inequalities of birth, wealth, or education as a common asset to be used for the benefit of all. With a few honourable exceptions, it regards them as the luck of the draw and the basis of personal gain. This assumption is so deeply embedded in our society that few people question it. It is assumed without debate that advantages of education, technical skill, professional status and the power to make decisions should entitle their holders to a markedly higher income.

Similarly, the conservative ideology cannot seriously regard ownership of capital or property as a secondary privilege, but treats it as an unquestioned right. It therefore finds great difficulty in preventing undue concentrations of economic power. It has little appetite for controlling the growing power of multinational companies, for example, and rarely sees any need to try.

Finally, because it takes inequality for granted, conservative ideology has little or no place for a downward redistribution of wealth and power. Individual conservatives may be deeply concerned about poverty, but do not connect it with their own wealth and social position. They practise a compassionate charity which relieves the worst distress and helps individuals to better themselves, but see no reason for redistribution, positive discrimination or other fundamental changes in the social structure. This ideology does not believe – and cannot afford to believe – that there is a vast reservoir of untapped ability and creative potential in the poor and oppressed. When forced into honesty, it rejects a fundamental equality of worth and defends the existence of hierarchies, elites, and serious social inequalities.

The conservative ideology's one defence against criticism has been that for all its faults, capitalism works, that it is efficient, and that it has been an unrivalled engine of development and material improvement. Speaking historically, this may of course be admitted, as Marx saw and admitted it long ago:

> The bourgeoisie, historically, has played a most revolutionary part … during its rule of scarce 100 years (it) has created more massive and more colossal productive forces than have all preceding generations together.[6]

Today, even apart from moral considerations and Marx's own detailed critique, the efficiency argument is increasingly open to question on other grounds. It is generally agreed that the whole dynamic engine of modern capitalism is fuelled by economic growth, by the development of new techniques, the discovery of more raw materials, the establishment of new markets and the production of more goods. The justification of the accompanying waste, alienation of people condemned to do monotonous work in which they can take no pride, and impoverishment of whole areas or populations, has been that in the long run some of the new wealth created would spill over from its creators to the rest of society. This belief is now being shaken in two ways.

Firstly, growth itself is in question. A long line of witnesses from every conceivable source is announcing that the writing is on the wall for our resource-eating, growth-dominated, high-consumption, northern–hemisphere way of life. We can no longer expect a future of unlimited economic growth on the present pattern. Experts differ widely on the limits of non-renewable resources and the extent to which nature can absorb industrial pollution, but there is a weighty consensus on this fundamental point. In the words of E. F. Schumacher, 'our affluent industrialised way of life cannot spread to all mankind and cannot last'.[7]

Secondly, even if environmental limits did not forbid it, and the patience of the poor permitted it, economic growth alone holds no solutions to poverty. Until very recently, Western economic theorists believed that it was in everyone's long-term interests to let the profit motive have free rein. Though only a minority could become rich, their wealth would accumulate capital for new investment, which could bring the whole economy to the point of 'take-off' into self-sustaining growth. The benefits of growth would then 'trickle down' from rich to poor, from the profit-makers to the job-seekers, from industry to agriculture, from the town to the village.

This doctrine may have had limited validity during a short period of European history, though it ignores the fact that Europe was first in the field and had the advantages of new markets, colonies, lack of competition, and new land for settlement which its expansion has necessarily denied to others. It is of doubtful validity in our own society today, where the most recent evidence suggests that there has been little or no improvement in the relative position of the poorest sections of the population.[8]

On a world scale, the 1960s showed that the trickle-down doctrine is an illusion. For while many economies grew rapidly, inequalities increased, both between rich nations and poor, and internally, within most Third World countries. Between 1960 and 1970 the total wealth of the world increased by £435,000 million, but 80% of that increase went to the countries where the richest quarter of the world's population live. In the same period, the lion's share of Brazil's remarkable increase in Gross National Product went to the richest members of its population. The share of national income received by the richest 5% *increased from 29% to 38%*, while the amount received by the poorest 40% of the population *fell from a mere 10% to 8%*.[9] Recent studies suggest that 'trickle down' is in fact 'trickle up' as far as the poorest citizens of third world countries are concerned.[10]

The efficiency argument with which conservative ideology defends its alliance with capitalism must therefore be questioned on its own ground. The waste of human talent, creativeness and ability among the poorest members of our own society, and in millions of people overseas, is hardly efficient, much less rational and humane.

*The 'liberal' view – freedom, justice, and reason*

The second major ideology ruled out by the understanding reached in previous chapters is the 'liberal' view. Again, this does not mean the policies of the British Liberal Party or its counterparts but a widespread attitude among all shades of political opinion.

Liberal ideology accepts many of the principles of social justice. In common with the conservative, however, it gives priority to freedom of the individual. Provided that it can remove the worst inequalities of birth and wealth, it believes that individuals should capitalize on their natural talents as best they can. It does not treat natural inequalities as a common asset and thinks of individual opportunity rather than responsibility to society. Usually, however, it accepts the need for some degree of redistribution and positive discrimination, and believes in a fundamental equality of worth.

The main defects in the liberal ideology are its attitudes to structural injustice and social conflict. The liberal sees the need for radical change, but is impatient with theories or grand designs. He prefers to tackle issues piecemeal, as they arise – to be pragmatic, and do what he can, where he can. He avoids the danger of theory divorced from action by opting for action without theory.

It is, of course, important to be down-to-earth, and to act. Yet where there is structural injustice, piecemeal action is unlikely to change it. I once visited a mission hospital in South Africa. It had a health care project whereby mothers of malnourished children were not given medicine, but shown how to prepare an adequate diet. Thus, they could see their children improve as a direct result of their own care. The project was an enlightened, imaginative piece of caring, one of many by its parent church.

The hospital is in the Transkei, one of the 'homelands' created by the policy of 'separate development'. This policy requires that all Africans live in their homelands, well away from the white cities. South Africa also pursues the goal of economic development – the growth and prosperity which give its white citizens one of the highest standards of living in the world. For this it is essential to have thousands of black Africans living near the cities, to work in the mines and factories and oil the wheels of industrial society.

The contradiction between the two aims is bridged by migrant labour. The black worker in the white city is treated as if he were a temporary sojourner who *really* lives in his distant homeland. Because he is 'temporary' he is forbidden to bring wife and children with him when the homeland's poverty forces him to come looking for work. Because he actually works in the city nearly all the time, he must live in near-permanent separation from his family. One and a half million African families are divided in this way, for up to ten months in the year. Family life breaks down, children never know their fathers, and wives and husbands seek companionship elsewhere.

The wives and grandparents cannot cope. The homelands are too small for the people who even now have to try and scratch a living from them – fourteen per cent of South Africa's land surface for over eighty per cent of her population. There is over-crowding, overgrazing, and consequent soil erosion. Children become malnourished, and grandparents are puzzled by the 'new diseases' of scurvy, kwashiorkor and pellagra which they never knew in their own childhood. They bring the children to the hospital, and the hospital does what it can to help.

The church which runs the hospital works on the liberal philosophy of piecemeal action. One might call it the philosophy of the given situation. It says, 'Given the situation of need, what can we do? Given that it is government policy to have home-lands, low wages, and migrant labour, how can we help those who suffer as a result?' It regards the structural relationships as outside its concern, and concentrates only on the immediate need.

In earlier times, when structural relationships were less clearly understood, or regarded as immutable, this was the only practical course. Today it borders on hypocrisy. For it is the white congre-gations supporting the mission hospital who benefit most from the suffering it relieves.

Though the example is unusually clear-cut, it has many parallels nearer home. Liberal ideology ignores the fact that a society is a total system, strong enough to absorb the tinkering of individuals. Caught up in the wider structures of injustice, the liberal humani-tarian says, in effect, 'Give service now, and let others worry about justice'. A more bracing slogan might be, 'Only those who work for justice have the right to offer charitable help.'[11]

Liberal ideology also shies away from the realities of power and conflict. Its abiding value – a belief in reason and goodwill – is also its gravest weakness. It sees consensus when it ought to admit dissensus, is reluctant to face the fundamental clash between the beneficiaries of injustice and its victims, and clings to the belief that it can stay serenely above the conflict between them.

The liberal desire to be neutral commonly appears in two related forms, especially in Christian circles. The first is an assumption that it is possible to give service to humanity which is unaffected by political ideology and motivated solely by brotherhood or Christian love.

Thus, a British charity's policy paper on aid to revolutionary movements argues that –

> We are in the great tradition of the Red Cross and other large relief bodies who uphold the principle, *no doubt derived from Christian roots*, that men are more than political animals, and that *to succour the afflicted is a universal obligation, without regard to political calculation.*

Accordingly, when whole areas of a country are in revolt against an established government, the charity in question refuses to take political sides. Its aid programmes to such areas are as uncontroversial as possible, though it accepts that the giving or refusal of aid is bound to have political implications:

> To imagine that any of our aid is totally without political consequences would be naive. To educate people, to help the poor to seize a new chance and realise their self-respect, even to keep people alive may well contribute to political changes. *The point we have to insist upon is that our aid is not given on a calculation of these political side-effects, but also that it is not withheld because of them.*[12]

Such policies are a valiant attempt to maintain political neutrality. Aid will not be given to revolutionary movements because they are trying to bring about fundamental changes like freedom from colonial rule. Nor will it be withheld because it might unwittingly help to bring about such changes as a 'side effect'. The problem is that structural changes are seen by the movements in question not as side-effects, but as the reason for their existence. To regard them as purely incidental is to make a political judgment, not remain neutral towards them.

Revolutionary movements are, of course, contentious and

ambiguous. It is a difficult matter of judgment whether a particular movement is likely to establish a more just society. To refuse ever to make such judgments or offer any challenge to the conscience of the church is not neutrality, but abdication. It is a political choice in favour of the conservative view that 'brotherhood' and 'Christian love' mean relieving distress and helping individuals to better themselves rather than changing an unjust social order.

The weakness of the liberal view is that nobody's understanding of brotherhood or Christian love is formed in a political vacuum. Consciously or unconsciously, anyone who uses such words does so, not in some pure or neutral way, but according to their understanding of how society works, what its main problems are, *and therefore of the way in which brotherhood or Christian love ought to be shown.* When they go beyond personal relationships, brotherhood and Christian love are inevitably interpreted through the tinted spectacles of an ideology.

This casts doubt on the second expression of liberal neutrality, the assumption that it is possible to stand outside all ideologies and criticize them without taking a political stand yourself. The tradition of academic objectivity has made an immense contribution to Western society. The problem is that the person who tries to make the detached criticism herself occupies a place in the structures of society, and cannot claim to be politically neutral towards them.

Thus, while detachment may be possible for the academic analyst, it becomes impossible as soon as he considers a specific political issue. When a church is faced with an oil company's plan to build a deep water terminal,[13] or when a charity wants to aid projects in areas controlled by a revolutionary movement, neutrality is impossible. The correct decision is not to try and cling to the illusion of neutrality but to make a conscious political choice and remain critical of it from within.

### *The 'socialist' view – equality, redistribution, conflict*

The third major ideological choice is, broadly speaking, socialist. A socialist ideology, like the other two, has at least three strands: some basic ideas of what a society ought to be; a general understanding of history, how change occurs and what stands in its way; and an analysis of particular economic and political structures leading to a detailed programme of action. The last element can receive only brief attention here. It varies considerably from country to country, and from one political group to another. In Britain, for example, there are important differences between socialists who seek change by parliamentary means and those who believe that such changes are more likely to come about through industrial conflict, workers' control or local community action.

As regards the first two elements, the previous line of argument undoubtedly points towards some kind of socialist ideology. All forms of socialism start from a belief in the fundamental equality of worth of every human being, and try to make that equality visible in society. A socialist ideology sees natural inequalities of ability, not as something to be levelled down or suppressed (a frequent misconception) but as a common asset, which must be developed to the full in *everyone* and used for the benefit of society *as a whole*. It rejects the free-for-all of conservatism and liberalism because, in practice, 'free-for-all' means 'freedom-for-some-at-the-expense-of-everyone-else'.

A socialist ideology therefore tries – by different methods and with varying degrees of success – to limit private ownership and to use goods, services, land and capital for the equal benefit of all. It takes redistribution and positive discrimination much further, and more seriously, than the liberal view. It has its historical roots in a passion for justice, a moral partisanship for the poor and oppressed.

Finally, of all the political choices open to the person concerned about justice, a socialist viewpoint is most clearly aware of the realities of power and the inevitability of conflict. Unlike the liberal, it does not expect history to be changed by moral persuasion alone.

The precise nature of the socialist alternative is a matter of analysis and political judgment. It cannot be settled by rational theory or drawn direct from the pages of the Old Testament. Though rational theory and Christian teaching call for redistribution they cannot say how it should be achieved. Israel's historical experience recognizes power as a key issue, and the abuse of power as at the root of social injustice. But it has no socialist alternative, and can only pray and demand that the kings, priests and elders do a better job of leadership. The same tradition also knows the necessity of conflict to win justice – Pharaoh does not let Israel go without a struggle, for example. But an experience of faith in pre-industrial society cannot be a guide to modern economic structures nor say how their conflicts could be resolved.

## *Radical socialism in outline*

To go into such questions in detail would be beyond the scope of this book. The line of argument in previous chapters does however rule out some versions of socialism and give important general guidelines for action. The principles of social justice do not, for example, allow us to do evil that good may come, or to sacrifice the bread of justice today for the jam of freedom tomorrow.[14] The goal of justice must be visible in the means used to achieve it, and should reach down into private life and personal relationships. We cannot work for justice through organizations, movements – or churches – whose internal structures are themselves unloving, oppressive and unjust.

Again, the line of argument in this book calls for a socialism based on dialogue. It is, of course, perfectly possible to find convinced socialists, and forms of socialism, which contradict their own principles by being dogmatic, domineering, and oppressive. Paulo Freire calls this attitude 'sectarian', and distinguishes it from the radical attitude which develops critical consciousness, always questions itself, and approaches other people as equals. The radical socialist does not go to people with slogans, nor tolerate tyranny and oppression. He maintains the dialectic between conviction and respect, and, even in the highest position of leadership, works *with* people, not over or for them.

Finally, because it knows the ambiguities of power and the limitations of human nature, radical socialism does not believe that the opposition between oppressors and oppressed is a clear-cut battle between the forces of light and the forces of darkness. In the most bitter and polarized struggle, the radical socialist does not allow herself the luxury of absolute righteousness. She knows that power will be a problem in the best socialist society. She lives in a constant tension between the conviction of being in the right and the perils of righteous indignation.

For the Christian, there is a corresponding tension between effective combat against injustice, and the command to 'love your enemies'. In the struggle for justice the Christian knows that he cannot be neutral. It is necessary to decide *for* some people and *against* others. The natural way of doing this is to love the people you are 'for' and be angry and hostile towards those you are 'against'. The limits of understanding between opposing groups[15] and the necessity of group solidarity make it difficult to love the class enemy.

Liberal Christianity resolves such tensions by denying the reality of the conflict. It clings to the belief that it can stay neutral, and be kind and peaceable to everybody. The socialist Christian will feel the tension acutely, but will be better placed to see the radical nature of the gospel command. For to love your enemies presupposes that you do have enemies, that you are in deep conflict with them, and that they have real enmity towards you. To love the enemy was never thought to be easy, but as long as it was a question of showing a certain sweetness of character it was preached without difficulty. 'In the context of class struggle today, *to love one's enemies presupposes ... that one has class enemies and that it is necessary to combat them. It is not a question of having no enemies, but rather of not excluding them from our love.*'[16]

# 10

# Is Justice Possible?

Where there is no vision, the people perish.

(Proverbs 29.18, AV)

It is better to light a candle than to curse the darkness.

Adlai Stevenson[1]

Can a just society be achieved? At the end of the argument, perhaps the greatest stumbling block to radical action is the world-weariness which hangs like a Los Angeles haze over Western industrial society, veiling the horizon and clogging the mind. The arguments may carry intellectual conviction, but the emotional response is that nothing can really change, that one social system is as bad as another, and that nothing we do will make much difference to our own society. It would be idle to think that such a deep-seated malaise could be adequately treated in a few lines, but three points may be made about it.

Firstly, it is open to question whether such feelings are universal. They contrast sharply with the hope, vigour and willingness to act and suffer which run like adrenalin through the veins of so many people and groups in the Third World.[2] Perhaps part of our world-weariness is the bafflement or guilt of the half-awakened oppressor. If so, it must be faced, accepted, and worked through. Dietrich Bonhoeffer said that the greatest half truth in Christian preaching was 'believe, and then you can obey'. He pointed out that for the earliest disciples of Jesus the two experiences came in reverse order. First they obeyed – they followed a man they hardly knew, much less regarded as Israel's Messiah. They took a first step of obedience, leaving behind the securities of fishing boats, homes, and extended-family support. Only after months of travel, talk, and action did they come to have faith. Education for justice gains its knowledge by action as much as thought. We may therefore have to obey in order to believe.

Secondly, the person who is convinced by the principles of social justice, but doubtful whether societies can be changed in any fundamental way, should look back through her own country's history, and give careful attention to other societies. In previous history, revolutions of one kind or another have occurred quite frequently. The intellectual history of science and the political history of Europe and North America show long periods of settled development punctuated by abrupt changes, overturnings of the political order or system of ideas. 'Revolution is the dialectical counterpart of evolution and development.'[3] It is not synonymous with violent conflict. It is not a disease of the body politic to be cured by better administration. It is an abrupt transition which is essential to growth. Our own society has changed in the past, often quite dramatically, and is changing rapidly today, under our very eyes. There is no reason to think that it cannot or will not change just as fundamentally in the future as in the past.

As to whether such changes can bring real improvement, it is important to weigh the evidence, and to question the judgments of our own news media, which inevitably interpret other societies from a liberal-conservative point of view. With memories of Stalinism, the Russian invasion of Czechoslovakia in 1968, and the oppressive treatment of dissidents and minorities by some socialist societies, there are ample grounds for caution. Yet there is also evidence that socialism has greatly improved the living conditions, personal fulfilment, and life chances of many people. China, Cuba, Yugoslavia, Poland, Tanzania and other socialist countries should therefore be looked at with fresh eyes. 'Many Christians will have many criticisms of this or that socialist country, but compare the USSR today with the old Tsarism, or Cuba of Castro with that of Batista, or today's China with the China of the Kuomintang, and you will find an *immense* release of human capacity.'[4] In my view there is enough truth in this statement to make a socialist society worth working for as the next step towards social justice.

A final point is that the motive power of education for justice must rest, not only on our expectation of what is possible, but also on a deeper vision and hope. The ideal of social justice is a permanent horizon which we may never reach. Yet we need such horizons if only to show us where we want to go, *to give significance to our journey*, and to release the inner energy needed to reach the next bend in the road. Social justice is a necessary ideal for people who want to be fully human, and to be true to themselves.

Christian hope will want to go further. Faith in Jesus Christ gives birth to the conviction that he has a continuing purpose for the world. If Christ is risen and alive, then the future is always open to hope, whatever the appearances may be. Alongside his concern for the eternal destiny of each individual, the God of righteousness works out his purpose for societies and their history. History is not a checker-board whose sole purpose is to turn individual pieces into kings and queens. It is a game of chess, where each individual move contributes to a total position, and where the outcome of the game matters as much as the fate of each knight or pawn.

In the New Testament, these convictions are presented not in a systematic philosophy, but in the word pictures of first-century faith. Thus, the individual Christian's earthly life can be seen as a house built on the foundation stone of God's work in Christ. The individual believer chooses her own materials and builds to her own design, whether badly or well. Her work will be 'tested to destruction', and may or may not survive, but the foundation remains.[5] On the other hand, the sickness in human society is portrayed by the figure of Anti-Christ, the final rebellion of evil before the final triumph of love.[6] The symbol stands as a warning against ideas of automatic upward progress. Social justice is worth working for because history shows real development and achievements, at ever higher levels of richness and complexity. Yet each new peak of achievement casts a longer shadow of distorted aims, evil possibilities, tragedy and disappointment. Both individuals and societies must come under judgment and be transformed. Thus, the book of Revelation sees the culmination of God's purpose as a resplendent city in a new creation. It is the dwelling place of individuals, but also a social unity, where people find life in fellowship with each other. It excludes everything unclean and is a realm where only perfection can dwell – yet it receives the achievements of world history, the wealth and splendour of the nations.[7]

The Christian who needs hope and strength to work for social justice will therefore reach back into the centre of her faith – to Jesus, the expression of God's love: crucified, powerless, dead, defeated and meaningless – yet in the same breath resurrected, creative, purposeful, resplendent and alive. She will combine self-acceptance with social responsibility, inner freedom with a hunger and thirst for righteousness. She will be reconciled and reconciling, the servant of others. Above all, she will live in a hope which rejects resignation as a false virtue[8] and struggles against injustice, even through weakness and failure, knowing that 'the only defeat is not to try'.

# Justice in Educational Methods

## *Some Ideas for Speakers and Leaders*

Education ought to be a dialogue between equal partners. It is however perfectly possible to believe in dialogue yet end up with educational methods or arrangements which are anti-dialogical, and therefore unjust. If we speak to our classes, audiences and congregations about dialogue and participation, but actually expect them only to listen, memorize what has been said, and ask the odd desultory question, the hidden message we are communicating (whether people accept it or not) is that passive acceptance is better than active learning, that reception is better than participation, and that knowledge or Christian truth are a package transmitted from us, who know, to the listener, who does not. Few teachers, leaders or preachers actually say such things. The message is communicated quietly and insidiously by the methods they use. Justice in education means understanding the hidden messages of behaviour, structure and techniques, and changing them so that they promote dialogue instead of hindering it.

### *Hidden messages of behaviour*

One aspect of behaviour is the use of language. For example, teachers and preachers often ask leading questions or make statements which the class or congregation are not expected to challenge – 'We like rhyming words, don't we?', 'These illustrations are very clever', 'What a profound thought that is in the words of our first hymn!' The implied message is that you *ought* to like rhyming words, and that you should accept the teacher or preacher's judgment instead of making your own. The form of words tends to discourage people from voicing their opinion, making their own act of knowing, or entering into a dialogue. It is not *really* envisaged that a child should reply 'No Miss, I don't like rhyming words', or that a member of the congregation should stand up and say, 'Well actually, vicar, I thought that hymn was terrible!' The solution is to monitor our use of language and develop a problem-posing style.[1]

A striking example of hidden messages comes from an American school arithmetic lesson. A student named Boris was at the blackboard. He had trouble reducing 12/16ths to its lowest terms and could only get as far as 6/8ths. The teacher was calm and pleasant towards him, but left him at the blackboard and told him to 'think'. As he stood there, tension mounted in the class. There was much heaving up and down of the other children, all frantic to correct him. At last, when Boris was unable to solve the problem, the teacher turned to the class and said, 'Well, who can show Boris what the number is?' A forest of hands shot up and the teacher called Peggy, who gave the correct answer.

In this episode, the excited hand-waving of the children indicates that they wanted to give the correct answer – but by definition this also entailed succeeding where Boris was failing. Despite her patience with the individual pupil, the teacher was using a procedure which encouraged the students to see education, and relate to each other, in a competitive way.[2] The hidden message being conveyed was that learning is an individual achievement in which some must fail in order that others can succeed. An alternative might be to encourage group work on such problems, and create situations which enable people to learn *from* and *with*, rather than against each other.

### The influence of furniture

A carpentry teacher once organized a course for building-trade craftsmen on the use of power tools and light machinery. On the first evening, the visiting lecturer found the students interested but unresponsive. No one would try the machines or ask questions. 'After an hour we went for a coffee and I tried to think where we had gone wrong. I realized that the chairs in straight rows made the class too formal. Even though most of the students knew each other they were inhibited by the formal presentation, so different from their own informal workshop practice.' A rearrangement of chairs, and the relaxed atmosphere over coffee, made the second half of the evening more successful – so much so that the class continued questioning, arguing, drilling concrete and cutting up timber for an hour after the scheduled finishing time.[3]

We all know from experience how the physical environment affects our behaviour. It is therefore vitally important to read the hidden messages of physical space, and especially of furniture arrangement and design. If straight-backed chairs are set round a table, the atmosphere of a group meeting is likely to be business-like. If armchairs are used without a table, it will be relaxed and informal. If the leader or teacher stands in front of a meeting seated in straight rows, the main talk-flow will be between leader and listeners. A semi-circular arrangement permits more talk among audience members, while a circle (in a small group) puts the leader on a par with everyone else. A compromise position is for the leader to sit at the end of a horse-shoe – part of the total group, yet visible to all and able to exercise leadership.

### Group size

The size of a group is another important part of the educational structure. Most familiar, perhaps, is the *face-to-face group*. This is the type of group most people are thinking about when they talk of having discussion groups or study groups. It consists of between eight and twelve people, with twelve as the maximum for effectiveness, and has three main characteristics.

Firstly, it encourages participation without demanding it. It is small enough for everyone to speak yet large enough for people to remain silent without feeling conspicuous.

Secondly, the face-to-face group encourages personal interaction – and therefore dialogue. Used over a period of time it can help its members to make honest and open relationships, work through conflicts and tensions, learn from, support and respect each other, and eventually change both their attitudes and behaviour. Such things do not happen automatically, but are most easily attainable in this size of group.

Thirdly, the face-to-face group encourages shared leadership. Its leadership tasks include: problem-posing, clarifying issues or procedures, presenting alternatives, picking up a neglected point, framing a possible decision, summarizing achievements, interpreting one member of the group to another, and showing interest and appreciation of other group members. In an established group such roles can alternate rapidly so that people give leadership who would otherwise remain shy and inarticulate.

The *small task-group* (often called a buzz-group, from the buzz of conversation when several such groups are operating) has a quite different pattern.[4] It consists of between three and five people, and works for a short time (between five and eight minutes) on a single specific task. Buzz groups are formed within a larger gathering by asking people to turn round and make groups of the required size. The task is explained, the time limit stressed, and the group immediately gets to work. Mixing can be aided by asking people not to sit with friends, or by asking pairs of people in one row to turn round and talk to the corresponding pairs behind.

The small size of such a group encourages every member to make some contribution, while the task and time limit concentrate the mind. It does not have the deep dynamics of the face-to-face group, and becomes boring or oppressive if left for too long a time. It does however allow maximum participation in even the largest meeting – since more people can speak in twenty groups of four than in one group of eighty. It allows people to share opinions, give a snap reaction, formulate a comment or question, recall what they have heard or seen, or list the points which they want the larger group to consider. The smallness of the group makes formally appointed leaders unnecessary, and allows members to sit close enough to hear each other – an important consideration in a noise-filled hall.

When buzz groups have met, the leader of the meeting collects their findings. If the meeting is small enough for everyone to see, the main points can be written briefly on paper or white board.[5] To save repetition the leader can take one point from the first group and link any similar points to it – thus bringing in a number of people fairly rapidly. The leader must avoid highlighting what she agrees with and neglecting what she dislikes, and should check that her summaries really capture the points made. When the collection process is completed the meeting moves on to discussion or analysis.[6]

A third important size of group is the *meeting* – by which is meant any educational gathering, including a formal 'class', of about twenty people or more. In a meeting, not all members can speak. Time prevents this, and the larger the meeting, the greater the restriction. Moreover, the sheer size of the meeting inhibits many people from speaking. Even in the most articulate gathering the absence of face-to-face contact makes many people feel exposed and anxious, less ready to risk ridicule or censure by their utterance – 'I can't sort out what I want to say quickly enough', 'I'd feel a fool, standing up among all these people', 'My question sounds so naive I'd feel daft to ask it' – these are common reactions. *It is therefore quite pointless to ask a meeting to have an open discussion unless its members have previously relaxed and gained confidence by meeting in smaller groups.*[7] Even then, the time-restriction will remain.

The best uses of a meeting are to debate or decide a particular issue, to thrash out issues raised by smaller groups, to conclude a longer session or programme, or to share a common experience as the basis for further work. Film, drama, role play, simulation games or a compelling speaker are shared experiences which release the normal inhibitions on contact with strangers. They enable people to meet each other and begin a dialogue. A classic example is the railway-carriage effect, when the train comes to an inexplicable halt and conversation replaces silence.

*From presentation to dialogue*

The scene is a Wives' Club on a Monday evening. Thirty people are seated in a pleasant hall on comfortable chairs. The chairs are arranged in straight rows facing a table, behind which are the chairwoman and guest speaker. After preliminary business, the chairwoman rises, welcomes the speaker, and gives the title of her talk. She notes the speaker's qualifications and experience, and promises that there will be time for questions. She is sure that everyone will learn something of value and is pleased to ask Mrs X to speak to us. Her introduction has lasted three minutes. She sits, and the speaker rises to warm applause. Mrs X then gives a well-presented talk lasting nearly half-an-hour. When she sits down, the chairwoman asks for questions. After a few moments' silence, the next fifteen minutes see a total of seven questions and four comments from six different members of the audience. The session is beginning to liven up when time runs out, the chairwoman thanks the speaker, and tea and biscuits are served.

Such events are still fairly representative of most people's educational thinking. They include the public meeting for the visiting lecturer with the big name, the Council of Churches meeting to hear from Mr B about the housing problem, the missionary supper with the Rev. Z or medical Doctor Y showing his slides, and the day conference which consists of three successive speakers followed by an hour of discussion groups, a reporting back session and a vaguely relevant film tacked on at the end.

To take the Wives' Club as an example, what are the messages being communicated by such a structure? The main message seems to be one of education-as-transmission. The speaker is cast in the role of authority – the person who knows. Her superiority in this respect is conveyed – despite the warmth and informality – by the chair arrangement (in which each individual audience member relates to the speaker rather than to her neighbours); by the existence of a speaker's table at a slight distance from the audience; by the format and wording of the introduction and vote of thanks; by the expectation that the speaker has the lion's share of the available time; and by a structure which allows only six people out of thirty to make a spoken contribution.

With very little trouble, even this unpromising medium can be altered to make it more dialogical. The simplest step is to allow more time for questions and use buzz groups immediately after the speaker's talk, asking each group to formulate one question or comment. The questions are either taken verbally or written down, passed to the chairman, and dealt with rapidly in order. Although the speaker is still the authority and focal point, this method increases participation by putting people, however briefly, in equal relationships with each other. This usually increases their willingness to participate thereafter 'from the floor'.

A further step towards dialogue is for the speaker to begin by asking the audience enabling questions[8] about the subject under discussion. When asked to speak about world development, for example, one can start by asking if anyone in the audience has been to a country outside Europe – and then where, how long and for what purpose. Or one can ask, in a general way, 'When you think of X, what are the first impressions that come to mind?' This is wide enough to cover facts, ideas, memories, mental pictures, opinions – anything, in fact, which the audience believes to be relevant. Debatable points can be thrown back in a problematizing way ('Does anyone want to add anything to this? Does anyone think differently about that?'). Even a large audience can become surprisingly involved, especially if the speaker shows interest and respect for *anything* that is said, and does not remain glued behind his table but moves about maintaining eye-contact with the audience.

From the speaker's point of view, this technique gives an invaluable insight into the expectations, possible misconceptions, and special knowledge of audience-members. From the audience's point of view it conveys the unspoken message that their experience and interests are important, that the speaker respects what they have to contribute, and that she welcomes their participation and even criticism thereafter. The audience members also learn something about each other.

After such a beginning, the speaker can more easily treat his own prepared talk in a dialogical way. The audience can be invited to listen in an enquiring frame of mind. One half can be asked (for example) to make a mental note of difficult or obscure points and be ready to raise them afterwards, while the other half can concentrate on points which need to be underlined or acted upon. After the talk, buzz groups can collect the reactions as a basis for discussion. A bolder method is to use buzz groups at the start and ask each group to list the main aspects of the theme which it would like to see covered. The resultant list becomes the framework of the speaker's talk, and a focus for later discussion.

*Time*

A major change made by all such techniques is to give more time to interaction and less to presentation. Similarly, it takes time for the face-to-face group to bring out the best in its members and change both attitudes and behaviour. To take education seriously means planning for dialogue and allowing adequate time for trust and openness to develop.

Such developments are impossible in a single meeting, however useful it may be in stimulating the interest of individuals. Many classes, conferences, and meetings seem unconsciously designed to *prevent* education. Their hidden message is – 'Don't worry. This will be pleasant and entertaining. You may even learn something new. But it won't involve you enough to make much difference to your life. And if it does challenge or disturb you, the effect will fade gracefully away by the time you get home'.

Time, then, is essential to dialogue. For dialogue demands of us the willingness to be changed by each other and by what we know. Such changes come from commitment and engagement with other people. They cannot happen overnight.[9]

# Notes

## 1. *The Act of Knowing*

1. Meaning not shyness, but awareness of one's self.

2. Pierre Teilhard de Chardin, *The Phenomenon of Man*, Collins and Harper & Row 1959, Fontana edition 1965. Some animals may have a degree of self-consciousness but the 'great divide' is real enough for the generalization to stand.

3. Neil Postman and Charles Weingartner, *Teaching as a Subversive Activity*, Penguin Books 1971, p. 82.

4. Ibid., p. 92.

5. I use the words dialectic/dialectical to refer, in a general way, to a *unity of opposites*, a clash of ideas or forces which are separate and opposed, but whose contradiction includes or can give birth to a deeper unity.

6. Quoted by Paulo Freire in *Cultural Action for Freedom*, Penguin Books 1972, p. 54.

7. *The Phenomenon of Man*, Fontana edition, pp. 35–37.

8. For many of the basic ideas in what follows, see Paulo Freire, *Education for Critical Consciousness*, Sheed & Ward 1974, pp. 3–5; *Cultural Action for Freedom*, pp. 51–57; and *Pedagogy of the Oppressed*, Herder & Herder 1970; Penguin Books 1972, pp. 70–73.

9. *Cultural Action for Freedom*, p. 43.

10. For a full description of the 'culture of silence' in Brazil, see *Education for Critical Consciousness*, pp. 21–23.

11. In this, too, humans differ from other animals. We would not speak of animals de-animalizing each other. Tigers do not de-tigerize other tigers.

12. Harry Salmon, *Hillfields – A Community comes Alive*, British Council of Churches, CRRU Pamphlet 1973, p. 9, emphasis mine.

13. *Cultural Action for Freedom*, p. 44.

14. Everett Reimer, *School is Dead*, Penguin Books and Doubleday 1971, pp. 143–144.

15. Arthur Koestler, *The Act of Creation*, Hutchinson 1964, pp. 121–124.

16. John Holt, *How Children Learn*, Penguin Books 1970, pp. 161–164.

17. Robert Holman, *Power for the Powerless: the Role of Community Action*, British Council of Churches, CRRU Pamphlet 1972, p. 15.

## 2. *Education as Dialogue*

1. *Teaching as a Subversive Activity*, p. 34.
2. Sir Derman Christopherson, *The University at Work*, SCM Press 1973, pp. 36–37, emphasis mine.
3. R. S. Peters, 'What is an Educational Process?', *The Concept of Education*, ed. R. S. Peters, Routledge & Kegan Paul and Humanities Press, New York 1967, p. 3 (emphasis mine). See also his essay, 'Education as Initiation' in *Philosophical Analysis and Education*, ed. Reginald Archambault, Routledge & Kegan Paul and Humanities Press, New York 1965, pp. 87–111.
4. Paulo Freire, in an unpublished letter to the Co-ordinator of a Cultural Circle in Chile.
5. Tom Lovett, *Adult Education, Community Development and the Working Class*, Ward Lock Educational Publications 1975, pp. 100–101.
6. D. Birt and J. Nichol, *Village Enclosure*, one of several such games published by the Longman Group Ltd Resources Unit, 9/11 The Shambles, York, England.
7. Culture in the anthropological sense. See above, pp. 4f.
8. So called because they allow the generation of the widest possible range of other syllabic combinations and of thought and discussion about the people's situation.
9. Clear, though slightly ungrammatical. Example based on Paulo Freire, *Cultural Action for Freedom*, pp. 29–47 and 85–88, and *Education for Critical Consciousness*, pp. 41–84.
10. *Cultural Action for Freedom*, pp. 24–25.
11. R. S. Peters, 'Education as Initiation', pp. 104 and 105.
12. Paulo Freire, *Education for Critical Consciousness*, p. 124.
13. Paulo Freire uses the terms 'teacher-student'/'student/teacher' (*Pedagogy of the Oppressed*, pp. 53ff.). I have modified this because in English the ideas of 'teaching' and 'learning' convey the opposition more clearly.
14. Paragraph developed from Neil Postman and Charles Weingartner, *Teaching as a Subversive Activity*, pp. 43–45 and Paulo Freire, *Education for Critical Consciousness*, pp. 124ff.
15. On this see *Education for Critical Consciousness*, pp. 150–155 and *Pedagogy of the Oppressed*, p. 54.
16. *Pedagogy of the Oppressed*, p. 62.
17. Ibid., p. 63.
18. Ibid.
19. *Letter to a Teacher by the School of Barbiana*, Random House, and Penguin Books 1970; Penguin edition pp. 95–97.
20. *Education for Critical Consciousness*, p. 55. Clear, though slightly ungrammatical.

21. *Pedagogy of the Oppressed*, p. 89, emphasis mine.

22. See note 10 to chapter 1, above p. 127.

23. *Education for Critical Consciousness*, p. 125.

24. Donald Bligh, *What's the Use of Lectures?*, Penguin Books 1972.

25. *Teaching as a Subversive Activity*, pp. 23–24.

26. Harry Salmon, *Hillfields – A Community comes Alive*, p. 12.

27. Bob Ashcroft and Keith Jackson, 'Adult Education and Social Action', *Community Work – One*, ed. D. M. Jones and M. Mayo, Routledge & Kegan Paul 1974, pp. 55–60.

28. Peter Marris and Martin Rein, *Dilemmas of Social Reform*, Penguin Books 1974.

29. R. S. Peters, *The Concept of Education*, p. 3.

30. R. K. Patterson, 'Social Change as an Educational Aim', *Adult Education*, vol. 45, no. 6, March 1973, p. 355.

31. *The Concept of Education*, p. 5.


## 3. *Justice in Rational Thought*

1. *It's Not Fair*, Suggestions for Junior School Assemblies, Christian Aid 1972.

2. I use the terms 'working class' and 'middle class' to describe the distinction between manual and non-manual workers. Though this may not be the most important class distinction to draw in Britain, Runciman shows that people still think it is, and that it still marks the sharpest distinctions of income and social status. See W. G. Runciman, *Relative Deprivation and Social Justice*, (1966) Penguin Books 1972.

3. Ibid., pp. 65–112.

4. Ibid., pp. 222–234. Recent research shows little apparent change in people's ranges of comparison. See Charles Elliott, *Inflation and the Compromised Church*, Christian Journals Ltd, Belfast 1975, pp. 29–45.

5. *Relative Deprivation and Social Justice*, p. 16.

6. The belief in some kind of fundamental human equality is deeply embedded in our culture. '. . . to criticize inequality and to desire equality is not . . . to cherish the romantic illusion that men are equal in character and intelligence. It is to hold that, while their natural endowments differ profoundly, it is the mark of a civilized society to aim at eliminating such inequalities as have their source, not in individual differences, but in its own organization' (R. H. Tawney, *Equality*, Allen & Unwin 1952, p. 49).

7. Example and quotation from Paul Ramsey, *Basic Christian Ethics*, SCM Press 1953, pp. 336f.

8. Lev. 19.15 (NEB), referring to the *administration* of justice in the Hebrew equivalent of law courts, the city gate. In *social* justice and policy, the poor are given preference. See chapter 4, below.

9. Government document quoted in *South Africa's Political Alternatives, Report of the Political Commission of the Study Project on Christianity in Apartheid Society*, Ravan Press, Johannesburg 1973, p. 15.

10. John Rawls, *A Theory of Justice*, Oxford University Press 1972.

11. The justification of this procedure is that a good metaphor or other concrete image can present ideas which would otherwise need several pages of abstract exposition. The two forms of speech are not interchangeable but can be complementary. See, among others, Max Black, *Models and Metaphors, Studies in Language and Philosophy*, Cornell University Press 1962. What follows is based mainly on the following pages of *A Theory of Justice*: 7–33, 60–192, 201–211, 243–251, 333–355, 424–446, 478f, 504–512, and 541–548.

12. Rawls' term: see *A Theory of Justice*, pp. 11–21 and 136–142.

13. Rawls' theory is a development of social contract ideas in the tradition of Locke, Rousseau and Kant.

14. Rawls uses the philosophical term 'goods', a 'good' being whatever from the viewpoint of a person or group satisfies its rational desires. I use the term 'benefits' to avoid confusion with 'goods' in the sense of 'commodities'.

15. Rawls argues that the two principles (which he sets out more fully on pp. 302–303 of his book) are to be taken in serial order, with the first having priority over the second. But this is only in the long run when 'a certain level of wealth has been attained'. Until that point is reached, restrictions on liberty in the name of equality would be permissible (*A Theory of Justice*, p. 542). This presents two difficulties. First, it assumes a society in continuous economic growth, and gives little guidance for the problems of living modestly within the limits of resources, population, food supply, etc. Secondly, since the order of priority only holds in the long run, it cannot serve as a standard or measuring rod in the forseeable future, once one considers the problems of justice on a world scale. Rawls only thinks in terms of the nation state – a curious and arbitrary restriction.

16. Gerald Dworkin, 'The Original Position', *Reading Rawls: Critical Studies of 'A Theory of Justice'*, ed. Norman Daniels, Blackwell, Oxford 1975, pp. 16–53. The principle of a fundamental equality of worth is an intuition about human nature which is the basis of the theory of justice as fairness, not a product of it. Rawls argues strongly against utilitarian approaches which deal with the *average* welfare of a society or of groups within it, and think in terms of 'satisfaction' or 'utility' rather than right.

17. For a full discussion of these points see the following essays in *Reading Rawls: Critical Studies of 'A Theory of Justice'*: Milton Fisk, 'History and Reason in Rawls' Moral Theory', pp. 53–80; Richard W. Miller, 'Rawls and Marxism', pp. 206–230; and Norman Daniels, 'Equal

Liberty and Unequal Worth of Liberty', pp. 253–281.

18. This may be described as a liberal view of society. See chapter 9, below, and Thomas Nagel, 'Rawls on Justice', *Reading Rawls*, pp. 1–16.

19. W. G. Runciman, *Relative Deprivation and Social Justice*, p. 322.

### 4. *Justice in Christian Faith*

1. Reinhold Niebuhr, *Moral Man and Immoral Society*, SCM Press 1963, p. 258 (first published in the USA by Scribner in 1932).

2. 'Pastoral Constitution on the Church in the Modern World' (cited below as 'Gaudium et Spes'), Section 26, printed in *The Documents of Vatican II*, Geoffrey Chapman 1967.

3. Ibid., Section 69.

4. Ibid., Section 26.

5. Ibid., Section 64.

6. St Thomas Aquinas, quoted by Thomas Cullinan, *The Roots of Social Injustice*, Catholic Housing Aid Society 1974, p. 9.

7. Pope John XXIII, in a Radio/TV message, 11 September 1962.

8. Papal Encyclical, *Mother and Teacher (Mater et Magistra)*, reprinted in Emile Guerry, *The Social Teaching of the Church*, St Paul Publications 1961, emphasis mine.

9. Charles West, 'Justice within the Limits of the Created World', *The Ecumenical Review* XXVII, no. 1, January 1975, pp. 57f.

10. *Our World and You*, Justice and Peace Commission 1972, p. 2. This is a simplified version of *Justice in the World*, statement by the 1971 Rome Synod of Bishops.

11. St Thomas Aquinas (see note 6 above).

12. *This is Progress*, Catholic Institute for International Relations 1969, Section 22. This is a simplified version of the Encyclical, *Populorum Progressio.*

13. 'Gaudium et Spes', Section 69. See also Guerry, *The Social Teaching of the Church*, p. 79.

14. Martin Noth, *Exodus*, SCM Press and Westminster Press 1962, pp. 102–120.

15. This fundamental experience was repeated and deepened in the conquest of Canaan, the ups and downs of national life under judges and kings, and the deliverance from exile in Babylon.

16. Deut. 10.17–20 (NEB).

17. Ex. 22.21–27.

18. Lev. 19.9–14, 18.

19. Isa. 11.5; 45.8; Amos 5.24; Ps. 85.10.

20. Jer. 22.13–19; Isa. 58.

21. Job 29.13–16 (NEB).

22. See e.g., Amos 2.6–8; 5.7, 10–15; 8.4–7; Micah 3.8–11; 6.9–12;

Isa. 10.1–3; Jer. 5.25–29.

23. E.g., Pss. 35 and 146.

24. Isa. 3.13–15 (NEB). For the nation as a vineyard see Isa. 5.1–7.

25. From the prophets' point of view, social injustice is bound up with religious apostasy. When the Israelites conquered Canaan, they settled down to till its fields, prune its vineyards and tend its flocks. Their nomadic faith in Yahweh leading his people through history clashed and mingled with local religions based on agriculture and the never-ending cycle of nature. The God of Sinai, with his passion for righteousness, became confused with the gods (Baals) of Canaan, whose main concern was the renewal of the flocks and the fertility of the fields. Thus, to worship Baal, or to see Yahweh in Canaanite terms, meant diluting the Covenant claims of righteousness. The frequent denunciations of idolatry, image-making and fertility rites should be seen in this light.

26. Amos 5.18–20; 7.7–8.3; cf., Isa. 28.14–22.

27. Jer. 32.1–25; Ezek. 37.1–14; Isa. chs. 40–55.

28. Isa. 54.6–10. The interplay between love and justice continues in the varied expressions of Israel's hope. Sometimes the justice of God is seen in a narrow and vengeful way: Yahweh will one day gather all the unclean nations, shatter them in a last great battle around Jerusalem and make them bring tribute to Israel. Others writers look forward to an era of universal justice and peace established by Yahweh's Servant or Messiah, or to a new creation of heaven and earth. See, e.g., Isa. 11.1–9; 42.1–4; 65.17–25.

29. Luke 19.5 (NEB).

30. A Jew would not believe in ghosts or hauntings: the shades of the dead were faded and powerless, imprisoned for ever in Sheol. The time-lapse alone, several years after the crucifixion, would rule out any idea of resuscitation.

31. See Romans, especially 1–3, 7–8.

32. John 12.32.

33. A valuable attempt to do this with regard to world economic changes is Charles Elliott, *Inflation and the Compromised Church*.

34. Amos 4.12f.; 5.1–3.

35. Matt. 5.6 (NEB).

36. Matt. 25.31–46, and compare Isa. 58.6–7.

37. Charles West, 'Justice within the Limits of the Created World' (see note 9 above), p. 61, emphasis mine.

38. John Rawls, *A Theory of Justice*, p. 334.

39. See note 1 above.

40. Thich Nhat Hanh, *Vietnam, the Lotus in the Sea of Fire*, SCM Press 1967, pp. 118f.

41. Gordon Zahn, *In Solitary Witness*, Geoffrey Chapman 1966, pp. 100f.

42. For an exploration of justice in educational structures and techniques, see the Postscript on pp. 119ff., below.

### 5. *Justice, Power and Conflict*

1. Reinhold Niebuhr, *Moral Man and Immoral Society*, pp. xxiii, xii, xv (extracts). Much of this chapter is based on Niebuhr's book.

2. Illustration taken from *The Village Game*, a simulation devised by the London Association for International Development, Ontario, Canada 1974.

3. *Moral Man and Immoral Society*, p. 28.

4. Glyn Roberts, *Questioning Development*, International Voluntary Service 1974, pp. 15–17. The following paragraphs draw on this work.

5. See note 1 above.

6. John Benington, 'Strategies for Change at the Local Level – Some Reflections', *Community Work – One*, pp. 267f.

7. Laurence Schlemmer, *Towards Social Change – Report of the Social Commission of the Study Project on Christianity in Apartheid Society*, Ravan Press, Johannesburg 1971, pp. 160f. The Study Project ('SPRO-CAS') was a joint programme mounted by the South African Council of Churches and the Christian Institute of Southern Africa between 1969 and 1973. Its aim was to apply Christian principles to every aspect of South African life.

8. Quoted by Stokely Carmichael and Charles V. Hamilton, *Black Power: the Politics of Liberation in America*, first published in the USA 1967, Penguin Books 1969, p. 14, emphasis mine.

9. Peter Marris and Martin Rein, *Dilemmas of Social Reform*, second edition, Penguin Books 1974, p. 73.

10. Richard Turner, *The Eye of the Needle*, pp. 3–8, and 'Teaching Social Justice', *White Liberation*, ed. H. Kleinschmidt, pp. 65–76, both SPRO-CAS publications, Ravan Press, Johannesburg 1972.

11. *Black Power*, p. 38, emphasis mine. Statistics cited include the following: black unemployment rates double those of white; 1965 unemployment higher for black high school *graduates* than for white high school *dropouts*; black postgraduates only able to earn as much as white high school leavers; ghetto merchants who daren't risk losses by giving credit and easy terms to impoverished customers so grossly overprice goods to be sure of their profit; and the majority of Chicago's ghetto blacks paying twenty dollars per month more for housing than their white counterparts elsewhere in the city; ibid., pp. 35–38.

12. *Moral Man and Immoral Society*, p. 210.

13. George Brager and Harry Specht, 'Mobilizing the Poor for Social Action', *Readings in Community Organization Practice*, Prentice Hall, New Jersey 1974, p. 226.

14. *Towards Social Change*, pp. 44f., 63, 160–161.

15. Ian Fraser, *The Fire Runs*, SCM Press 1975, p. 27.

16. *Dilemmas of Social Reform*, p. 287.

17. John Benington, 'Strategies for Change at the Local Level', p. 266.

18. A further conclusion is that there is a fundamental difference between individual and group morality. While individuals may accept the ideal of service, organizations, institutions and nations usually take what they can get. Thus, the highest ideal for individual morality is unselfishness, but for group morality the highest ideal must be justice. It is wishful thinking to believe that the love of sacrificial individuals or the small community can ever be extended to encompass all human-kind. Even if every individual in a nation became totally unselfish that nation would still lack love in its dealings with others, since the individuals within it could never gain enough understanding of another nation's point of view to guarantee that their own national behaviour towards it was totally loving and just. See *Moral Man and Immoral Society*, pp. 9, 51–82, and 259.

## 6. *The Marks of Cultural Oppression*

1. See above, pp. 64f.

2. *Towards Social Change*, p. 30.

3. Paulo Freire, *Education for Critical Consciousness*, pp. 1–84.

4. Paulo Freire, *Pedagogy of the Oppressed*, pp. 39 and 37.

5. *Education for Critical Consciousness*, pp. 120f.

6. George Brager and Harry Specht, 'Mobilising the Poor for Social Action', p. 224.

7. John Dearlove, 'The Control of Change and the Regulation of Community Action', *Community Work – One*, pp. 23–26.

8. Name given to inter-tribal clashes in South Africa, e.g. in the compounds of male hostels.

9. *Pedagogy of the Oppressed*, p. 40. See also Peter Marris and Martin Rein, *Dilemmas of Social Reform*, pp. 79f. and Frantz Fanon, *The Wretched of the Earth*, Macgibbon & Kee 1965.

10. Jules Henry, *Essays in Education*, Penguin Books 1971, pp. 43–50.

11. There are about two million 'Coloured' people in South Africa, mixed-race descendants of intermarriage.

12. *Moral Man and Immoral Society*, p. 118. The Coloured Representative Council was at the time of writing a consultative body intended to represent the interests of the Coloured population.

13. One Dutch Reformed Church Pastor told me he sincerely believed that his church had been given a divine call to leadership in Southern Africa, to bring the light of Reformed faith to the dark continent, but

it is open to question how far such convictions are now widespread.

14. *Moral Man and Immoral Society*, pp.117f.

15. Ibid., p. 125.

16. Home Office document quoted in *The National Community Development Project Inter-Project Report*, CDP Information and Intelligence Unit 1973, p. 1. The following paragraphs draw on this source.

17. This and the preceding quotation are from Home Office documents quoted in the *Inter-Project Report*, p. 1 (see previous note).

18. *The National Community Development Project Forward Plan 1975–76*, CDP Information and Intelligence Unit, May 1975, p. 2.

19. Ibid., p. 23.

20. Ibid., p. 38.

21. *CDP Final Report Part I – Coventry and Hillfields: Prosperity and the Persistence of Inequality*, CDP Information and Intelligence Unit March 1975, pp. 17f.

22. *Inter-Project Report*, p. 8.

23. Peter Marris and Martin Rein, *Dilemmas of Social Reform*, pp. 103 and 124f. Their judgment is based on a careful analysis of programme resources, schemes and employment statistics.

24. Harry Salmon, *Hillfields – A Community comes Alive*, p. 15.

25. It is a general human trait to take our attitudes from our own group and, through ignorance or fear of the stranger, to see members of other groups in stereotypes and generalizations. Because the oppressor has power over the oppressed, his stereotypes of the oppressed person do more damage than the oppressed person's stereotypes of the oppressor.

26. See above, pp. 69ff.

27. *Moral Man and Immoral Society*, p. 129.

## 7. *Awakening to Justice*

1. Everett Reimer, *School is Dead*, p. 96.

2. Ernest Baartman, *The Significance of the Development of Black Consciousness for the Church*, unpublished address to the South African Methodist Conference, 1972.

3. In Britain it is customary for both the professional and voluntary educator to separate educational situations clearly and decisively from 'politics' or 'activism'. If education for justice gains its new knowledge as much by action as by reflection (chapter 1, above) such a sharp separation is clearly impossible. In fact, the relationship is dialectical. One can neither divorce the intent-to-learn of an educational situation from the committed action of a political campaign nor merge one with the other. Education for justice is 'a practical education: it comes through action, participation and vital contact with the reality of injustice'. (*Justice in the World*, Statement by the Rome Synod of Bishops, 1971, p. 19.)

4. 'Conscientization could never be an imposition on others or a manipulation of them. I cannot impose my conviction on someone else. I can only invite him to share, to discuss.' (Paulo Freire, in a recorded talk on conscientization, Rome 1970.)

5. See above, pp. 20ff.

6. Paulo Freire, *Pedagogy of the Oppressed*, p. 39. (The reference is to Allende's Chile, before the 1973 Military Coup.)

7. Ernest Baartman, *The Significance of the Development of Black Consciousness* (see note 2 above). Baartman believes that black consciousness has its roots in the work of Christian missionaries leading to a black awakening to the significance of the doctrine of every person's creation in the image of God.

8. *The National Community Development Project Forward Plan*, p. 2.

9. Anne Power, *I Woke Up This Morning*, British Council of Churches, CRRU Pamphlet 1972.

10. Ginsburg, quoted by Robert Holman, *Power for the Powerless*, p. 10.

11. See note 18, chapter 5, above p. 134.

12. For this reason Paulo Freire rightly argues that *fundamental* change can come only at the initiative of the oppressed. The beneficiaries of injustice cannot, as a group, bring justice to its victims. For a similar conclusion following a detailed study of the economies of several Third World countries, see Charles Elliott assisted by Françoise de Morsier, *Patterns of Poverty in the Third World*, Praeger 1975.

13. G. Müller-Fahrenholz, 'Overcoming Apathy', *The Ecumenical Review* XXVII, no. 1, January 1975, pp. 55f.

14. On SPRO-CAS see note 7 to chapter 5, above p. 133. The quotation is from Clive Nettleton, 'The White Problem', *White Liberation*, ed. H. Kleinschmidt, pp. 8f. The Afrikaaner Nationalist Party has dominated the white Parliament in South Africa since 1948 and is the chief architect of *apartheid*. A proverbial saying is that many whites talk Progressive, vote United Party and thank God for the Nationalists.

15. H. Kleinschmidt, ibid., p. 2. The words in brackets in the second quotation are added, emphasis mine.

16. For a clear yet profound Christian interpretation see Thomas Cullinan, *Coping with Bafflement*, Christian Aid *Viewpoint* Paper, 1971.

17. Dimbaza is a 'Resettlement Township' in Cape Province, South Africa, to which aged and unemployed 'superfluous Bantu' are endorsed out from urban areas on the grounds that they are unproductive and really belong in their notional 'homeland'.

18. Reinhold Niebuhr, *Moral Man and Immoral Society*, p. 33.

19. Paulo Freire, in a recorded talk on conscientization. See note 4 above.

## 8. *Learning the Realities of Power*

1. Both quotations are from *Community Work – One*, pp. 31 and 88.

2. Martin Luther King, *Why We Can't Wait*, Signet Books, New York 1964, pp. 84f.

3. See chapter 6 above.

4. What follows is developed from two articles in *Readings in Community Organisation Practice*, 'Disruptive Tactics', by Harry Specht, pp. 372–386, and 'Types of Purposive Social Change at the Community Level', by Roland Warren, pp. 205–222.

5. Even where disruptive tactics are the main weapon, rational approaches like debate and information-gathering are also needed, to convince the target of action that the changes demanded are less disturbing than it believes, or that the consequences of not changing are likely to be worse and more damaging, than the consequences of change.

6. Harry Specht, *Readings in Community Organisation Practice*, p. 227.

7. *Community Work – One*, p. 267.

8. Using the Americanism in preference to UK 'co-option' because 'cooptation' now carries this specialized meaning in community work literature.

9. *Community Work – One*, p. 38.

10. Peter Marris and Martin Rein, *Dilemmas of Social Reform*, p. 329.

11. Ibid., p. 353.

12. Keith Jackson, 'The Marginality of Community Development – Implications for Adult Education', *The International Review of Community Development*, Summer 1973.

13. *Dilemmas of Social Reform*, pp. 346ff., emphasis mine.

14. Ibid., p. 345.

15. See, for example, the magazine, *Community Action* and its 1975 *Investigator's Handbook*, and the research reports of Counter-Information Services.

16. Bennie Khoapa, 'The New Black', *Black Viewpoint*, ed. B. S. Biko, SPRO-CAS Black Community Programmes, Durban, South Africa 1972, p. 64.

17. Ernest Baartman, *The Significance of the Development of Black Consciousness*.

18. Albert van den Heuvel, 'Living in Conflict', *The Expository Times*, LXXX, June 1969, pp. 273–276.

19. Martin Luther King, *Why We Can't Wait*.

20. For a full discussion see United Reformed Church, *Non-Violent Action*, SCM Press 1974.

## 9. *Taking a Political Stand*

1. Quotation from *Frontier*, June 1972, p. 75, from an article also drawn on in the rest of this chapter.

2. Bob Ashcroft and Keith Jackson, in *Community Work – One*, p. 47.

3. Ken Coates and Richard Silburn, *Poverty – the Forgotten Englishmen*, Penguin Books 1970, conclusion on pp. 232–235. See also Keith Jackson, 'The Marginality of Community Development – Implications for Adult Education' and Peter Marris and Martin Rein, *Dilemmas of Social Reform*, passim.

4. There is extensive documentation on these questions including church reports in the USA, the work of Counter-Information Services in London, the Fifth Report from the House of Commons Expenditure Committee (1973–74) on wages and conditions of employees of British companies in South Africa, and the research reports of Christian Concern for Southern Africa and War on Want.

5. Archbishop Helder Camara, *Structures of Injustice*, Justice and Peace Commission 1972, p. 5.

6. *The Communist Manifesto*, 1848.

7. A random selection includes Barbara Ward (*The Angry Seventies*, Justice and Peace Commission 1970 and, with René Dubos, *Only One Earth*, Penguin Books 1972), Robert McNamara (World Bank President, in speeches from 1970–1974), Robert Heilbroner (*The Human Prospect*, 1974), the UN Conferences on the Environment (1972), Natural Resources, Population and Food (all 1974), and the World Council of Churches five year multi-expert study on Science and Technology for Human Development (Report published, 1974, in the journal, *Anticipation*, no. 19, 'The Ambiguous Future and the Christian Hope').

8. See Charles Elliott, *Inflation and the Compromised Church*.

9. Statistics taken from *Christian Aid in the World of 1973*, a Christian Aid briefing leaflet, and *An Address to the UN Conference on Trade and Development*, 1972, by Robert McNamara, President of the World Bank Group.

10. Limitations of the trickle-down model in Third World countries include the fact that their rich minorities do not necessarily save and invest but spend their surplus on foreign travel and imported consumer goods in order to reach the life-style of the affluent countries. For a well-argued economist's view see Samuel Parmar in *Fetters of Injustice*, World Council of Churches 1970. On 'trickle-up' see Charles Elliott and Françoise de Morsier, *Patterns of Poverty in the Third World*.

11. Adapted from José Miguez Bonino, *The Ecumenical Review*, XXVII, no. 1, January 1975, p. 43.

12. Christian Aid Board Paper, 1975, emphasis mine.

13. See above, pp. 66f.

14. The trickle-down theory of capitalism does this, of course, quite as brutally as some versions of Marxism.
15. See above, chapter 5.
16. Gustavo Gutierrez, *A Theology of Liberation*, Orbis Books 1973 and SCM Press 1974, p. 276, emphasis mine.

## 10. *Is Justice Possible?*

1. At the funeral of Eleanor Roosevelt.
2. See the many examples in Ian Fraser, *The Fire Runs*.
3. The quotation, and the interpretation of revolution and development, are from Arend Theodoor van Leuwen, *Development through Revolution*, Scribner, New York 1970, a profound and wide-ranging work which deserves to be better known in the UK.
4. James Klugmann, 'Communism – the Future', *What Kind of Revolution? – A Christian-Marxist Dialogue*, ed. James Klugmann and Paul Oestreicher, Panther 1969, p. 174.
5. I Cor. 3.10–17.
6. II Thess. 2.1–4. See also the symbol of the Beast in the book of Revelation.
7. Rev. 21–22.
8. *Manifesto to the Nation*, Bolivian Methodist Church 1970, *Viewpoint Paper*, Christian Aid.

### *Postscript: Justice in Educational Methods*

1. Jules Henry, *Essays in Education*, p. 107.
2. Ibid., p. 172.
3. Ron Parker, News Item in *Teaching Adults*, March 1974, p. 10.
4. The following paragraphs are based on my article 'Buzz Groups', in *Teaching Adults*, February 1974.
5. Chalk on blackboard is acceptable though less vivid. Large lower-case lettering is more easily read at a distance than capitals, which is why it is now used for motorway signs.
6. To summarize, the essential points about buzz groups are:
(*a*) *Size* The upper limit of five is vital. Larger groups should be tactfully broken up. A group of six or more cannot do a concentrated *task* and inevitably becomes a slower-moving discussion.
(*b*) *Task* This must be clear, simple, and specific. For example: 'List up to four points you now want to make', 'Draw up two questions or comments', or 'Decide which of the three courses of action you would prefer us to follow'. Buzz groups cannot cope with more than

one task at a time.

(*c*)  *Time*  The short time limit (maximum ten minutes) is essential to get a quick and concentrated response. It is best to announce that groups will have five minutes, allow eight, and quietly warn groups when they have only a minute left.

(*d*)  *Collection*  The results must be collected quickly, fairly, and comprehensively, so that people do not feel cheated or ignored.

7.  This point also applies to church congregations, and for the same reasons.

8.  See above, pp. 21f.

9.  For further exploration see the following:

Jennifer Rogers, *Adults in Education*, BBC Publications 1973.

Paul Bergevin, Dwight Morris and Robert M. Smith, *Adult Education Procedures – A Handbook of Tested Patterns for Effective Participation*, The Seabury Press, New York 1963.

*Games and Simulations*, BBC Publications 1972.

# Index of Names

# Index of Subjects

Apathy
  of oppressors, 84f.
  of the poor, 6f., 72, 76f., 81, 87

Black consciousness, 79, 82, 136

Capitalism, 105–107
Christian Institute of Southern Africa,
  85, 99f.
  SPRO-CAS programme of, 130,
    133f., 136, 137
Codification, 18, 80
Conflict, social, 40f., 57
  exposure of, 90
  levels of, 91f.
  liberal attitude to, 110f., 114
  and love of enemies, 113f.
  meaning of, 65f.
  mirrored by inner conflict, 84
  and reconciliation, 98f.
  resolution of, 59, 93
  unavoidability of, 65f., 87, 113
  of vested interests, 58f.
  between victims and beneficiaries of
    injustice, 67f.
Conscientization, 80–89, 128, see also
  Education for Justice
Consensus, 91f., 110
Cooptation, 95f., 137
Critical consciousness
  development of, 10f., 80
  and education for justice, 31, 55f.,
    62, 79
  and ideology, 103, 113
  nature of, 5f.
  political implications of, 81
Culture, 4f., 19f., 25, 57f., 79, 128
  'cultural circle', 17, 70–72
  cultural oppression, 6f., 69–81
  cultural power, 61f., 65, 87f.

'culture of silence', 71, 127
'Cycle of deprivation', 74–76

Economic development
  goal of, 43
  no solution to poverty, 107
Economic growth, limits to, 44, 106,
  130
Education
  as dialogue, 12, 17, 20–29, 55f., 71,
    80, 84, 86f., 119–126
  definition of, 27
  for justice, 6f., 11, 31, 56, 62, 68,
    79–81, 83f., 116f., 135
    must itself be just, 55f., 80, 119
  and learning, 7–11, 120
  by memorization and repetition,
    19f., 27, 119
  not neutral, 29, 56, 80
  and political action, 135
  by problem-posing questions, 13–
    25, 71, 80, 84, 119
  of teacher and learner, 13, 20–25, 26
  as transmission, 12, 20–29, 80, 119,
    123f.
Educational structures
  furniture and physical space, 120f.
  group size, 121–123
  hidden messages of, 119–121, 124,
    126
  language, 119f.
  time, 126
Equality, 32, 33, 40, 98, 129, 130
  in education, 15, 20f.
  of liberty, 38
  of opportunity, 40, 55
  of power, 62, 68
  of worth, 40, 41, 43f., 51, 55f., 67f.,
    77, 80, 105, 108, 112, 113, 130